Satisfied

How God Can Meet
Your Deepest Needs

Mark Finley

Pacific Press® Publishing Association
Nampa, Idaho
Oshawa, Ontario, Canada
www.pacificpress.com

Editing and page design by Ken McFarland
Cover art direction and design by Michelle Petz

Copyright © 2002 by
Pacific Press® Publishing Association
Printed in the United States of America
All Rights Reserved

Additional copies of this book may be purchased
at http://www.adventistbookcenter.com

World Edition
ISBN: 0-8163-1973-1

02 03 04 05 • 4 3 2

Contents

1. On Our Own 5

2. Developing a Winning Attitude 17

3. Empowered by the Spirit 29

4. Luther's Greatest Legacy 39

5. Eyewitnesses of the Unbelievable 53

6. An Advance on Eternity 65

7. Still Standing Tall 79

8. A Family Against the Odds 95

9. The Best Is Yet to Come 107

10. Jesus Satisfies Our Every Need 125

I need to know I'm not all alone
and on my own.

On Our Own

IT WAS A GIANT in the energy industry—the seventh-largest corporation in the United States and one of the most innovative and admired. Enron amassed huge profits in the '90s by wheeling and dealing in natural-gas pipelines, electric plants, and water companies. It made the most of utilities deregulation. By 2001 Enron stock was valued at more than 60 billion dollars.

A golden thread runs through the stories recorded in Scripture about the heroes of faith. Through all the ups and downs of their lives, they pursued an intimate relationship with God through faith, and they were fully satisfied.

Then—total collapse. Stockholders woke up to find the company swimming in debt and its market price plunging. In January of 2002, Enron stock had lost 99 percent of its value. Thousands of Enron employees were out of work—and feeling betrayed.

How did it happen? How did dazzling prosperity

turn into such a disaster—and so fast? Shockwaves from the largest bankruptcy in United States history have swept over us all. We are left to wonder what we can count on. Is there any source of security when the mightiest among us fall so hard?

During the early fallout from the collapse of the Enron Corporation, *Time* magazine came out with a cover that said it all: "You're on Your Own, Baby."

That was the conclusion of writers and researchers who looked into everything from brokerage firms to phone companies to HMOs.

Start with the scariest news about Enron. No one, it turns out, did anything to protect the interests of ordinary stockholders.

Executives left them on their own. As the crisis built, they sold off their own Enron stock while telling everyone else the company was doing just great.

Board members left them on their own. They were deeply involved in some of the shady deals that would bring Enron down.

Auditors left them on their own. They had a vested interest, it turns out, in disguising the bad news about the company.

Regulators left them on their own. They failed to blow the whistle on a company that was hiding huge amounts of debt.

So people who'd worked for the company for years—people whose 401(k) plans were tied to Enron stock—suddenly found themselves out of a job and out of a retirement plan. Small-time investors lost everything, while millionaire executives cashed out. You're on your own. That's part of the fallout from the Enron disaster.

And there's more, as *Time* points out. You're on your own when it comes to stock analysts and financial planners. They're often getting a commission from companies they're urging you to buy into. Sometimes they get paid more for selling you shaky stocks than solid ones.

You're on your own when it comes to medical care, *Time* says. You have to navigate through the complex options of an HMO, a PPO, or a POS. Hospitals and insurers are looking at the bottom line. No one is trying to get you the best care at the best price.

You're on your own when it comes to phone companies, they add. After deregulation, there are all kinds of companies competing for local service, long-distance service, cellular service, DSL, cable modems, satellite links, and other telecommunications services. The service plans are complicated. You almost have to have a math degree just to figure out what a local call is going to cost you.

You're on your own. That's the conclusion analysts have come to after looking over the present landscape. It's a landscape under the shadow of Enron's collapse, of course—what *Newsweek* magazine called "a total system failure."

No one's looking out for you. That's the feeling people are getting these days.

Well, I would like to respectfully disagree. I respectfully disagree with *Time* and with all the analysts who tell us, "You're on your own, baby."

I do agree that the landscape has changed. I do agree that many companies aren't as solid as they would like us to believe. I do agree that you have to check things out very carefully for yourself when making large financial investments.

But I don't agree that we're on our own. In fact, nothing could be further from the truth.

Today, I want to tell you why I believe we're not on our own. And I want to demonstrate that fact through some individuals who accomplished great things, who looked back on their lives, and who said with one voice, "I was not alone." I think their testimony is powerful and persuasive. It's especially powerful in these times when the foundations are being shaken all around us.

First, let me present as evidence a man named Moses. Let's consider his recollections in the book of Deuteronomy. Deuteronomy is, in a way, the *Memoirs of Moses.* He's an old man looking back on a lifetime of incredible adventure. He began his career at a time when his people, the children of Israel, were enslaved by the mightiest empire of that era—the empire of Egypt. Times were pretty dark.

But this is what Moses wrote at the end of it:

"Therefore know that the Lord your God, He is God, the faithful God who keeps covenant and mercy for a thousand generations with those who love Him and keep His commandments."—Deuteronomy 7:9, NKJV.

God comes through. That was Moses' conclusion. He keeps His promises. He's faithful. He's consistent— for a thousand generations.

Now, mighty Enron had a spectacular run for, what, maybe ten years? That company rode the crest for a decade and then crashed, bringing down countless dreams with it.

The God of heaven, on the other hand, will remain steadfast through an entire generation—your generation—and He will do the same through your children's generation, and your grandchildren's generation, and your great-grandchildren's generation. He's in a different ball game!

Now, please notice this. Moses wasn't a man coming up with nice sentiments about God in an ivory tower. He was writing after a life of conflict, after struggles and hardships in a wilderness, after trying to lead a fickle group of ex-slaves toward the Promised Land.

Through all those experiences, he came to know— and know for sure—that "the Lord your God is the faithful God who keeps covenant."

Listen to Moses' conclusion about God:

"He is the Rock, His work is perfect; for all His ways are justice, a God of truth and without injustice; righteous and upright is He."—Deuteronomy 32:4, NKJV.

Do you feel afraid when a financial powerhouse like Enron collapses? Do you feel unsure when the great energy empire it built up suddenly seems as flimsy as a shredded document?

Please remember the God who faced down the power of Egypt. Remember the One who took on the Egyptian Empire through His servant Moses.

A series of well-aimed plagues brought stubborn Pharaoh to his knees, and all of Egypt with him. But the Almighty stood tall. He stood tall because His work is perfect, because His ways are justice, because He is a righteous God.

In the world right now, it's pretty hard to guess which company is going to stand and which company is going to fall. It's hard to trust the numbers—after Enron. But you don't have to guess about God! You don't have to guess about who will be the last man standing.

The God of heaven is someone you can depend on—to a thousand generations. He's the reason you're not on your own.

Let me show you another bit of evidence. This comes from a general, looking back on a life of struggles and battles. It's Joshua, the man who led Israel into the land of the Philistines, the land of promise.

Listen to what he said in his farewell address:

"And you know in all your hearts and in all your souls that not one thing has failed of all the good things which the Lord your God spoke concerning you. All have come to pass for you; and not one word of them has failed."—Joshua 23:14, NKJV.

In all of Israel's ups and downs there was one constant—the Word of God. Not one thing failed in all that He promised. Not a word had to be taken back. That's the testimony of a soldier named Joshua.

You know, Enron promised a lot of good things for its stockholders. It kept saying good things right up until the end. In its last annual report, executives made this promise to customers: "Enron's ability to deliver is the one constant in an increasingly complex and competitive world."

Constant? The real constant at Enron was simply profit. In August of 2001, an Enron executive assured employees in an email that the company was on solid footing. But during the same period, according to *Time,* he was trying to sell his own way out of the mess by exercising options.

False assurances. Empty promises. Words that just weren't backed up. That's what thousands of laid-off Enron employees are looking back on, with a bitter taste in their mouths.

Friends, God's words aren't like that. God's words don't let us down. Joshua stood up to bear witness that not one of God's words failed. And countless others join him.

Listen to the prophet Isaiah:

"The grass withers, the flower fades, but the word of our God stands forever."— Isaiah 40:8, NKJV.

That's another reason I can say to you, even in times like these —you're not on your own. Someone is looking out for you. Someone has made promises you can trust.

But there's still more evidence. Let me tell you about the testimony of a man who'd been through real tragedy—utter disaster. Ezra had seen Israel collapse. He'd seen an addiction to idols sap his nation's moral strength. He'd lived in exile in Persia after the destruction of Jerusalem.

But Ezra saw God come through on His covenant with Israel, even after they turned their backs on Him. Following a remarkable series of providences, the Hebrew exiles returned to their land. Cyrus, the king of Persia, actually enabled them to begin rebuilding Jerusalem!

Standing there in the City of David, Ezra looked back over some very stormy decades and said this:

"For we were slaves. Yet our God did not forsake us in our bondage; but He extended mercy to us in the sight of the kings of Persia, to revive us, to repair the house of our God, to rebuild it's ruins, and to give us a wall in Judah and Jerusalem."—Ezra 9:9, NKJV.

God came through—even in the worst of times. That was Ezra's conclusion. He came through when we were at our lowest. He came through when we'd given up hope.

Do you remember what happened to Enron when it first hit bad times? What happened when investors first caught sight of the debt the company had been hiding? Abandon ship! That's what happened. People dumped Enron stock as fast as they could. Enron executives had already been selling off their stock—abandoning ship, in effect—right before running it aground.

The price of Enron stock took a nosedive. And suddenly everyone in sight was rushing to distance themselves from the company.

Regulators, bankers, politicians, stock analysts—everyone tried desperately to cut off the Enron connection. Legislators who'd had cozy chats with Enron executives suddenly hardly knew their names. Congressional staff members got busy tracking down campaign contributions from Enron—and giving back the money!

No one wanted to be anywhere near the Enron collapse. You're on your own. Watch your back. Don't know anything about it. Those were the watchwords of the day.

But those are not God's policies. That's not how God treats us when we're down. He doesn't run away from disasters. He picks us up. He binds our wounds. He breathes life into hopeless cases. There's a story of a man who had a dream about his life. He looked back on it as a series of footprints in the sand. There were two sets of footprints, side by side. That was evidence of God walking beside him through the years. But at one particularly low, dark place, one set of footprints disappeared. Troubled, the man asked God, "Why did You forsake me when I needed You most?"

God replied, "That's when I was carrying you."

Friends, companies rise and fall. Stocks soar and then plunge. Banks make mistakes. Regulators sometimes fail to regulate.

But the God of Moses, the God of Joshua, the God of Ezra—He's not going to fail. He's going to carry us through the tough times.

The apostle Paul discovered that. He's another voice raised in testimony to the God who is with us. He'd been through a lot of hardships in his missionary travels around the Mediterranean. But he came to a wonderful conclusion:"Who shall separate us from the love of Christ? Shall tribulation, or distress, or persecution, or famine, or nakedness, or peril, or sword? . . . Yet in all these things we are more than conquerors through Him who loved us. For I am persuaded that neither death nor life, nor angels nor principalities nor powers, nor things present nor things to come, nor height nor depth, nor any other created thing, shall be able to separate us from the love of God which is in Christ Jesus our Lord."—Romans 8:35, 37-39, NKJV.

That's what Paul saw, looking back. It's one of the most inspiring statements about life ever uttered. On our own? Paul would have chuckled about that. He'd experienced a love so strong, so persistent, that nothing in heaven or earth could break it.

But Paul would also tell us something else. He would also tell us that, although God's love is always with us, we're not always with God's love. We can close ourselves off from it—even as it's staring us in the face.

"The goal of this command is love, which comes from a pure heart and a good conscience and a sincere faith. Some have wandered away from these and turned to meaningless talk."—1 Timothy 1:5, 6, NIV.

It's possible to turn away from love. It's possible to wander away from a sincere faith. It's possible to let idle chatter, trivial pursuits, and the busy-ness of life get in the way of God's love.

The truth is, so many people feel they're on their own—because they've left God alone. God is with us, but are we with God? That's the question. He's invested everything in us. What have we invested in Him?

God can't really manufacture a relationship with us all on His own. He needs our involvement. Listen to Paul again:

"Some people, eager for money, have wandered from the faith and pierced themselves with many griefs."—1 Timothy 6:10, NIV.

Wow! What an accurate diagnosis of life in the post-Enron world. People zeroed in on making money at all costs. They wandered from principles of honesty. They wandered from principles of fairness. And yes, they were pierced with many griefs. Those stocks that just kept rising suddenly became a down arrow that went right through them.

There's an important principle we need to remember in a world where so many think they're on their own. When faith fades away, greed always rushes in to fill the vacuum. Faith connects us to the God who's always there, the God who takes care of our real needs. Without that vital connection we feel empty. Something's lacking—there's a hole we need to fill. So we try to get more things to fill that hole. We acquire more, accomplish more, conquer more. We taste success. But the hole's still there.

The leaders of Enron weren't satisfied when their company became a big player in the energy game. They weren't satisfied when their company started earning millions. They weren't satisfied when they started earning billions. They weren't satisfied when they made more money than they could spend in a couple of lifetimes. They had to acquire more. They had to make more deals. They had to keep scheming and plotting.

When faith fades away, greed always rushes in to fill the vacuum.

You don't want that to happen in your life. That's why I urge you today to respond to the testimony of Moses; respond to the testimony of Joshua; respond to the testimony of Ezra. Respond to what the great men of faith are telling you about life. Respond to the challenge the apostle Paul brings us. God has invested everything in you. What have you invested in God?

Please remember, people feel they're on their own, when they leave God alone. It's time to take steps in the other direction. It's time to be there for the God who's always there for us. It's time to pursue the one thing that can truly fill us up. It's time to pursue a relationship with God with all our strength, and all our mind, and all our hearts.

TWO

I need less fear and more faith.

Developing a Winning Attitude

IN THE FIFTEENTH CENTURY a motto of the Spanish Empire was *ne plus ultra*—"no more beyond." With their vast empire, the Spanish kings and queens assumed there was no more to conquer. They believed their explorers had gone to the ultimate, discovering everything to be discovered.

Caleb and Joshua were motivated by the positive spirit of faith rather than the negative emotion of fear. They were fully satisfied with a God much, much bigger than their problems.

Then came Columbus. In 1492 he discovered a new world, and the old motto was outdated. The great explorer had discovered more beyond.

Some people's lives get stuck in a rut. They live as if there were no more beyond. They become stagnant. They have stopped growing. They no longer stretch themselves. They live within the narrow circle of their thoughts. Their minds are closed to anything but their own opinions.

Joaquin Miller has written a magnificent short poem on Columbus. He describes the explorer's attitude in these lines:

> *Behind him lay the gray Azores,*
> *Behind the gates of Hercules;*
> *Before him not the ghost of shores,*
> *Before him only shoreless seas.*
> *The good mate said, "Now we must pray,*
> *For lo, the very stars are gone,*
> *Brave admiral what shall I say?"*
> *"Why say, sail on, sail on and on!"*

Sail on and on and on! What a life attitude—a winning attitude!

Whatever you know about any subject, there is more to learn. However proficient you are at anything, you can become even more proficient. Whatever you have discovered, there is more to discover. Whatever you have learned, there is more to learn.

We hear this ring of Columbus's words echoing down the centuries—sail on—sail on—sail on.

◆ Sail on in the face of obstacles.

◆ Sail on in the face of difficulties.

◆ Sail on in the face of problems

◆ Sail on in the face of opposition.

◆ Sail on in the face of criticism.

◆ Sail on in the face of doubt.

◆ Sail on in the face of fear.

◆ Sail on in the face of defeat.

◆ Sail on in the face of mistakes.

The Bible character who perhaps models this spirit of a winning attitude in the face of enormous obstacles more than any other is Caleb. Here is the setting.

Israel is at the borders of the Promised Land, camped at Kadesh-Barnea.

Moses chooses twelve men—all leaders—to quietly slip into Canaan and under the cloak of secrecy spy out the land.

"Go from here northward into the southern part of the land, then into the mountains. Find out what the land is like, what kind of people live there, whether there are many or few and how strong they are. Find out what the country itself is like. What kind of towns do the people live in? Are they open cities or are their cities fortified? What is the soil like? Is it fertile or not? How much of the land is wooded and how much is open field? And bring back some of the grapes that grow there."—Numbers 13:17-20, The Clear Word Bible.

The spies' investigative analysis was to be thorough. Israel's attacking armies must be fully informed. A positive report would spur them on to a courageous conquest. They did their task well. The spies carried out their assignment carefully. They explored the land for forty days, then returned home.

They gave a glowing report. They excitedly told of a land that was rich and fertile with an abundance of fruit. They "showed off" a cluster of grapes so heavy that it took two men to carry it hanging from a pole between them. They also displayed baskets of figs and pomegranates.

The Israelites were ecstatic. Canaan was more fantastic than they imagined. It was beyond their wildest dreams.

The spies continued their report. "But . . . there are problems . . ."

◆ The people who live in Canaan are giants—powerful warriors.

◆ Their cities are large and protected with high walls.

◆ They are all descendants of Anak, the giant.

◆ The Amalekites live in the south.

◆ The Hittites, Jebusites, and Amorites live in the mountains in the north.

◆ The Canaanites are scattered along the Jordan River.

"We will never defeat them. The place is full of giants. We felt like grasshoppers next to them. There is no use trying. There is only one solution. Let's go back to Egypt. The best thing to do is return. Let's choose another leader who will take us back."

Enter Caleb and Joshua. Caleb speaks:

"Let's not be afraid to go up and take the land! Look at what God can do. Look at what He has done already! With His help we can do it." (See Numbers 13:30; 14:8, 9.)

What a contrast! Two very different attitudes:

◆ One says, "It can't be done!" The other says, "Let's do it!"

◆ One says, "We will be defeated." The other says, "We will overcome."

◆ One says, "We can't." The other says, "We will."

One thing is certain—if you tell yourself long enough that you cannot, you will not! If you tell yourself long enough that you are a loser, you will lose. If you repeat it often enough, no matter how untrue, it will become reality to you.

What was the primary difference between Caleb and Joshua and the ten other spies? Here it is in a nutshell:

The ten were paralyzed by fear. Joshua and Caleb were motivated by faith. In Numbers 14:24, God Himself describes Caleb in these words:

"My servant Caleb . . . has a different spirit in him and has followed Me fully."—NKJV.

What is the different spirit that enabled Caleb to follow the Lord fully? It is the positive spirit of faith—NOT the negative emotion of fear.

"It was Caleb's faith that gave him courage, that kept him from the fear of man, and enabled him to stand boldly and unflinchingly in defense of the right. Through reliance on the same power, the mighty General of the armies of heaven, every true soldier of the cross may receive strength and courage to overcome the obstacles that seem insurmountable."—*Review and Herald,* May 30, 1912.

Faith connects us with the divine power of the Creator of the universe. Through faith, we receive strength and courage to overcome insurmountable obstacles.

Fear and faith are opposites.

Fear sees the worst. **Faith** believes the best, and even if the best becomes the worst, faith finds a way through.

Fear insinuates doubt. **Faith** grasps God's hand and believes.

Fear retreats. The fearful Israelites cried out, "Let's go back to Egypt."—See Numbers 14:3. **Faith** advances. Caleb shouted, "Let's go up and take the land!"

Fear regards the unknown as a threat. **Faith** regards the unknown as a challenge.

Fear seeks comfort from the past. **Faith** seeks the opportunities of the present.

Fear wants the known, the predictable, the status quo. **Faith** delights in the adventure of the unknown.

Fear sees the obstacles. **Faith** seizes the possibilities.

Fear cripples, paralyzes, stifles. **Faith** liberates, frees, enables.

Fear sees what is and trembles. Faith sees what can be and rejoices.

Fear focuses on and exaggerates the problem.
Faith sees beyond the problem and looks to the God who can solve it.

Fear sees problems as bigger than God. **Faith** sees God as bigger than any problem.

Fear infects others with the virus of doubt. **Faith** inspires others with the serum of hope.

Fear tends to blame God for the problem. **Faith** trusts God through the problem.

Faith is believing God—trusting Him. It is a settled confidence in Him. It moves at His command. It obeys at His word. It walks in His strength and lives in His power.

Joshua, Caleb's buddy, cried out:

"Be strong and of good courage; do not be afraid, nor be dismayed, for the Lord your God is with you wherever you do."—Joshua 1:9, NKJV.

Someone has said, "Courage in people is like a tea bag. You never know their strength until they are in hot water."

This life-giving faith does not give up when the going gets tough. Faith is not some hyped-up emotional do-goodism. It is not some kind of do-it-yourself psychotherapy. It is not:

◆ Faith in yourself.

◆ Faith in your abilities.

◆ Faith in your skills.

◆ Faith in your talents.

It is faith in God.

◆ The God of the universe—the God of the sun, moon, and stars.

◆ The God who says to the tides, "Stop here—go no farther," and they stop.

◆ The God who says to the sun, "Rise," and it rises.

◆ The God who says to the rain, "Fall," and it falls.

◆ The God who says to the flowers, "Bloom," and they bloom.

◆ The God who says to the wind, "Blow," and it blows—and "Stop," and it stops.

The reason faith produces such courage is because it is rooted in the infinite power of God.

Faith enables you to have the courage to scale the highest peak and climb the most rugged mountain. It did for Todd Huston.

Todd set the world record for climbing the highest peak in each of the fifty states. The previous record was 101 days. Todd shattered that record handily by completing his 50 climbs in 66 days, 22 hours, and 47 minutes. His toughest climb was Mt. McKinley in Alaska.

Mt. McKinley rises out of the Alaskan range to a majestic elevation of over 20,000 feet—the highest point in North America. Its jagged peak lies just three and a half degrees south of the Arctic Circle.

The mountain is perpetually covered in a shroud of snow and ice.

Climbers who have attempted the ascent know that the mountain's moods are capricious and unforgiving. Mt. McKinley remains one of the most challenging climbs in the world.

Todd had to maneuver across huge crevasses and around avalanches. He had to pass over the glaciers jutting up against the mountain, and he had to endure constant exhaustion and cold.

One of Todd's biggest tests came when he met a group of climbers on their way down from Mt. McKinley.

"What's it like up there today?" Todd asked.

One of them shook his head. "Bad storms and high winds. We were locked in at Denali Pass for three days."

Todd asked eagerly, "But did you make it to the summit?"

The man shook his head. "The summit loses its significance in the face of survival. I am just happy to get off that mountain alive."

Todd Huston had to make a choice. Was he going to try it? Was he going to take on this tremendous obstacle with only one leg? You see, Todd had lost his leg in a boating accident while water skiing when he was only fourteen years old. The boat's gears jammed in reverse, and the propellers on the engine mutilated his leg. To save his life from the infection which later set in, Todd's leg was amputated just below his knee.

Todd's faith and courage led him to set the world

record for the fastest time in climbing the highest peaks in each of the fifty states.

Sometime ago, I interviewed Todd on *It Is Written* television. I asked him how he was able to climb the mountains he climbed—not only the physical ones but the tremendously challenging mountains of discouragement, disillusionment, fear, frustration, difficulty, and disaster he faced.

Todd's answer was right to the point.

"If you are going to look at your affliction or your injury and focus on that, you are going to live around it. But if you focus on the Lord, He is just going to get you through it. It's going to be a learning experience. You are going to move on and become wiser and stronger because of your mountain."

◆ Faith conquers mountains of difficulty.

◆ Faith scales the heights.

◆ Faith soars into the heavens.

In a phenomenal display of courage, when he was eighty-five years old, Caleb said:

"Now give me this mountain. Bring on the giants. Show me the walled cities. The Lord and I will conquer them."—See Joshua 14:12.

"The unbelieving had seen their fears fulfilled. Notwithstanding God's promise, they had declared it was impossible to inherit Canaan and they did not possess it. But those who trusted in God, looking not so much to the difficulties to be encountered but to the strength of their Almighty Helper, entered the goodly land."—*Patriarchs and Prophets,* p. 513.

At eighty-five years of age, Caleb cried out, "Give me this mountain!"—and God gave it to him.

Full of energy, possessed with the vitality of a man forty years younger, eighty-five-year-old Caleb led the armies of Israel into battle. The old man's army attacked and overthrew the giants. They conquered an apparently unconquerable mountain.

My reading friend, I want to challenge you—no matter what you may be facing in life at this moment—to go out and, by faith, take your mountain. You may have before you mountains of problems to be solved, difficulties to unravel, challenges that seem to defy solutions.

You may be facing . . .

◆ Mountains of despair.

◆ Mountains of hopelessness.

◆ Mountains of defeat.

◆ Mountains of heartache.

◆ Mountains of sorrow.

◆ Mountains of broken dreams and shattered hopes.

◆ Mountains of seemingly unconquerable habits and unsolvable problems.

The world is looking for positive, pro-active people who leap into the world's need and with courage say, "Give me this mountain!"

The world is looking for people who don't flinch when they are faced with obstacles. The world is look-

ing for people who don't cave in at every little difficulty.

By faith in the Almighty power of the living God
and with a heart filled with courage, take on your mountain and sail on—and on—and on—and on—and on!

THREE

I need the power of Christ's personal
presence in my life.

Empowered
By the Spirit

IT WAS A VIOLENT LAND in a violent time,
and they were violent men.

It was an immoral land at an immoral time, and they
were immoral men.

It was a pleasure seeking land in a pleasure-bent
generation, and they were pleasure-seeking men.

Violence, lust, and pleasure seeking walked hand
in hand throughout the land.

John the Baptist's straight-forward message thunders across the centuries. There is nothing more satisfying than to immerse your life in the warmth of God's presence.

The rich oppressed the poor,
and the poor battled one another to eke out a meager existence. Nothing seemed to really satisfy. Their hearts were
empty. Their souls were barren.
Abandoning all restraints, they
lived only for the moment. They lived by no standard
but their own. Their restless, guilt-ridden hearts
plunged them only further into pleasure seeking.

But deep down inside—in the inner recesses of the

heart where it really matters—they were empty. They longed for something more. They were restless and needed peace. They were guilty and needed forgiveness. Their hearts were spiritually hungry, and they needed to be satisfied. Their wills were weak, and they needed strength. They were confused and needed direction.

Then he appeared. A bearded, straight-talking, no-nonsense prophet clothed in camel's hair, preaching in some remote place by a river called the Jordan.

He was not part of the religious establishment. He had no titles, degrees, or prominent position. He was certainly not some nationally known TV evangelist or radio speaker, not the dean of a school of theology or chairman of a religion department. He wasn't some prominent religious leader or officer of the church.

But this one thing he had: POWER. He was anointed by the Holy Spirit, and when he spoke, lives were changed. When he spoke, they fell to the earth and cried for mercy. When he spoke, it was as if people were standing in the presence of God. They came by the thousands to hear his words of repentance, cleansing, and new life. This man ripped aside all the pretense and sham of religion. He spoke directly to their hearts.

They called him John—John the Baptist.

His message penetrated deep. His message hit home. His message convicted their consciences. His message transformed their lives. Compelled by the Spirit, they entered the Jordan and were baptized.

He spoke in the first century, but his message speaks to us again in the twenty-first century. He spoke at the beginning of the Christian era, but his message speaks to us still at the end of the Christian era. He spoke to prepare men and women before the First Advent, but his message speaks to prepare men and women for the Second Advent.

"I indeed baptize you with water unto repentance," John preached. "But He who is coming after me is mightier than I, whose sandals I am not worthy to carry. He will baptize you with the Holy Spirit and fire." —Matthew 3:11, NKJV.

What is the baptism of fire? Consider with me the symbolism of fire in the book of Exodus.

◆ The fire of the burning bush—Exodus 3:1-4.

◆ The fiery Shekinah glory—Exodus 25:22; 24:17.

◆ The pillar of fire by night—Exodus 40:38.

From these verses, it's clear that the fire represented the warmth of God's personal presence. The Holy Spirit is the personal presence of Christ. And John calls for authentic Christianity—the presence of God in one's life.

Speaking of the Spirit to come, shortly before His departure from this earth, Jesus told His followers, "I will not leave you comfortless: I will come to you." —John 14:18, KJV. The word *baptism* means "immersion." So the baptism of fire is immersion in the presence of Christ.

John's is a call for genuine, authentic Christianity. This is no call for something artificial. This is no call for the "outer" without the "inner." This is a call for an inner heart experience with God.

Now, as we look back over the history of the Christian church—over some of the mountaintop periods of Christian history, we find one such mountaintop in the experience of the Celtic Christians of the fourth and fifth centuries. They grasped the reality of the presence of Christ.

In recent years, there has been a revival of interest in Celtic Christianity.

◆ Celtic songs.

◆ Gaelic folk dances.

◆ Celtic customs.

And recent years have also brought a rediscovery of the fervor of Celtic Christianity.

Early Celtic Christians had a sense of the presence of God in their lives. Their hymns and poems and prayers reflect their deepening godliness—this personal encounter with God. In the fourth and fifth centuries, the Celts preserved some of the features of early New Testament Christianity.

As a grade-school student, I attended St. Patrick's Catholic Grammar School.

Little did I know that Patrick of Ireland was a committed, Bible-believing Christian—and most likely a Sabbath-keeping Christian too. It's clear that Patrick grasped the significance of the baptism of the Spirit and fire. He saw it as the presence of God in one's life—as immersion in God's presence.

Not long ago, I read a prayer that summarizes to me

the essence of this Celtic Christianity, called "St. Patrick's Breastplate":

Christ be with me, Christ within me.
Christ behind me, Christ before me.
Christ beside me, Christ to win me.
Christ to comfort and restore me.

Christ beneath me, Christ above me.
Christ in quiet, Christ in danger.
Christ in the hearts of all who love me.
Christ in the mouth of friend and stranger.

The prayers of the early Celtic Christians reveal the possibility of friendship with God. They reveal this focus on total immersion in the presence of Christ. Here's another Celtic prayer:

I am bending on my knee
In the eye of the Father who created me,
In the eye of the Son who purchased me,
In the eye of the Spirit who cleansed me,
In friendship and affliction.

Early Celtic Christians longed to be immersed in the personal presence of Jesus Christ! John's call for the baptism of fire is a call for genuine, authentic Christianity which is more than an intellectual understanding, more than a theological correctness. John appeals not for sham, not for pretense, not for lip service, not for superficiality. He appeals instead for spiritual depth, for genuine spirituality. He appeals for friendship with God.

Baptism by fire is immersion in the warmth of God's

presence. And I believe God is calling you and me today to experience the presence of God in a deeper way. I am convinced that we who follow Jesus are being called to something deeper—that we're being called into the warmth of the presence of God.

Fire is a symbol of God's personal presence. But it is also a symbol of His purifying presence. Fire is a symbol of the presence of the Spirit of God who burns up the dross in your life—the chaff in your life. "But who can endure the day of His coming? And who can stand when He appears? For He is like a refiner's fire."—Malachi 3:2, NKJV. So there is a work of purification that God desires to do in our lives.

Not long ago when I was in Madras, India, to preach, I got up one morning and looked out the window. I couldn't see a thing. Smoke surrounded our hotel. Smoke was filling my room. I went out into the lobby—more smoke. My heart began beating fast, and I said to myself, "This hotel may be on fire!"

Quickly, I ran downstairs and went to the front desk and asked, "What's going on? I smell smoke!"

"Oh, Pastor Finley, didn't anybody tell you?" they replied. "On January 14, we have the Hindu festival of burning."

"What's that?" I asked.

Now, Madras has about 13 million people, and in the Hindu culture, once a year, they look at anything that might be cluttering their lives: old clothes, old furniture, and other items. And on the annual festival of burning, they take anything that they consider to be cluttering their lives and burn it up, to purify their lives.

Have you ever faced the daunting task of cleaning out all the "stuff" and clutter from your garage? I wonder if it's possible that our lives can become so cluttered with "stuff" that we just take it all for granted. What about supposedly harmless gossip? What about the risqué TV programs you might watch when no one else is around? What about dishonesty? Unfaithfulness in tithing?

You see, the baptism of fire has to do with the Holy Spirit convicting us in our own personal life—convicting us of lust and greed and pride, of arrogance, of selfishness. The baptism of fire has to do with an inner purification. We are living at a time in earth's history when sin is tolerated, both in the world and in the church. And in the name of tolerance and understanding, almost nothing is considered really wrong today. No moral compass. No "north star" to guide us. Adultery becomes "my private business." Drinking becomes socially acceptable, even for Christians. Lying becomes my own perspective. Gossip and character assassination become cloaked under the veil of "concern."

What is the plague spot in your own soul? What door is God knocking on in *your* heart?

After David's shameful sin with Bathsheba, he came to God and cried out for a deep, cleansing work of God in his life:

"Create in me a clean heart, O God, and renew a steadfast spirit within me. Do not cast me away from Your presence, and do not take Your Holy Spirit from me."—Psalm 51:10, 11, NKJV.

David longed to have the lustful thoughts, the adulterous leanings, the wandering eyes cleansed. In bare-faced repentance, David openly acknowledged his sin.

Yes, the baptism of fire symbolizes a deep, heart-felt, genuine work of inner purification. But there are also times in the Bible when the term "baptism of fire" represents a baptism—an immersion—in fiery trial.

Notice what Jesus Himself said: "I came to send fire on the earth, and how I wish it were already kindled! But I have a baptism to be baptized with, and how distressed I am till it is accomplished!" —Luke 12:49, 50, NKJV. The baptism that Jesus was to be baptized with was the fiery trial of the Cross. Judas would betray Him. The disciples would forsake Him. Peter would deny Him. The Jews would ridicule and mock Him. The Romans would crucify Him. Jesus would go through loneliness, rejection, heartache, disappointment, and sorrow. He would endure physical pain—a crown of thorns jammed down on His head, nails driven through His hands and feet. Jesus would pass through the fiery trial—the baptism of fire—of the Cross.

The baptism of fire is the personal presence of Christ in your life, the purifying presence of Christ to cleanse you from sin, and the powerful presence of Christ to be with you as you pass through trials. His power makes it possible for trials to come and leave you better, not bitter. His power can result not in scars, but in helping you shine as one of His stars. The fiery trail does not consume you. Your greatest trials can become your greatest joys. You are broken only to be made beauti-ful for the kingdom of God.

Are you going through some great trial in your life now? Some fearful financial difficulty? Some health problem? Some marital problem? Some overwhelming loss or grief? What is your fiery trial? The baptism of fire in your life may very well be the baptism of a fiery trial. But in that fiery trial, we can see the presence of Christ.

"Therefore," Peter wrote, "since Christ suffered for us in the flesh, arm yourselves also with the same mind, for he who has suffered in the flesh has ceased from sin [a life of sin—not the act of sin], that he no longer should live the rest of his time in the flesh for the lusts of men, but for the will of God."—1 Peter 4:1, 2, NKJV.

You see, Christ suffered every single thing that you and I go through. And when we go through our fiery trial, Jesus goes through that trial with us! In that fiery trial, we find the presence of Christ. We find our faith strengthened in that fiery trial. We find ourselves drawn nearer to Christ in that fiery trial.

In the fiery trials of life, when down seems up and up seems down, we need the baptism of the Holy Spirit. In the fiery trials of life, we need to know that at times God uses trials to purify us—that though God doesn't cause them, He can use financial reverses, and sickness, and divorce, and so many other trials to purify us and get us ready for heaven.

And faith means that I trust God in the midst of my fiery trial. It means that I trust Him in all my difficulties. It means that I understand that Christ, too, lived in this world and experienced loneliness and sorrow and disappointment and pain and heartache. It means that I know that whatever I go through, Jesus has gone through, too.

John the Baptist's message continues to speak to you, my friend. Have you had a superficial Christian experience? God wants to baptize you with fire so that the presence of Christ fills your life. Have you become tolerant of sin? God wants to baptize you with fire so that He can purify your life. Are you going through some fiery trial? He wants you to know that He is refining you in that trial—and that He is with you in that trial every step of the way.

FOUR

I need to feel secure about my salvation.

Luther's Greatest Legacy

THE DOOR OF THE Castle Church in the town of Wittenberg, Germany, once shook with the hammer blows of a young priest, pounding a placard into place. Printed on the notice were 95 theses—95 points he was making and offering up for public debate.

Martin Luther discovered freedom from the accusing voices which had haunted him for years—and an inner peace through Christ's incredible gift of salvation. Experiencing God's amazing grace, he was fully satisfied.

The author, Martin Luther, was protesting against indulgences—the offering of forgiveness for sale. And his small act of protest was the first step in one of the most significant religious revolutions of history.

But more important, this revolution brought to light a wonderful solution to a basic human dilemma, a dilemma we still struggle with today.

In 1517, Luther, a young parish priest at the Castle

Church in Wittenberg, noticed that more and more people walking down the town's streets were carrying certificates in their hands.

Luther found out that they had procured these certificates in a neighboring city, where a Dominican friar named Tetzel had set up a special sale of indulgences.

People thought that indulgences were, essentially, a way to tap into the accumulated merits of the saints. It was believed in the Middle Ages that their righteousness could be transferred to believers who came up short. And this could help ensure one's entrance into heaven.

At first, indulgences were given to those who made certain pilgrimages or performed special works of piety. But later, they were offered to anyone who made special contributions to the church.

And in Luther's day, the pope was trying to build St. Peter's Cathedral in Rome. He needed an enormous amount of money. So an enormous number of indulgences were offered to those who contributed. In other words, forgiveness was for sale.

This was too much for this young priest, and he was moved to nail up his placard at the Castle Church.

What many people don't know is that there were many other individuals who protested against the corruption of the church in Luther's day. Many other people tried to reform the church. But they failed.

Why did Martin Luther succeed? Why did he become such a giant in the history of the church?

Where did he find the leverage to move the colossal power of the church?

Here in the shadows of the Castle Church in Wittenberg, Martin Luther made a discovery. He found something in the Bible that transformed his life. He found a truth so strong and sure and solid that it gave him security and confidence even in the midst of continual attacks by church officials.

Luther's great discovery came while he was preparing for a series of lectures at Wittenberg University on the book of Psalms. Luther came across Psalm 22. He was struck by the prophetic picture of Christ's sufferings. He read these words: "My God, My God, why have You forsaken Me? . . . The congregation of the wicked has enclosed Me. They pierced My hands and My feet; I can count all My bones. . . . They divide My garments among them, and for My clothing they cast lots."—Psalm 22:1, 16-18, NKJV.

Luther began to think about why Christ had repeated those words on the cross—"Why have You forsaken Me?"

Jesus wasn't weak. Nor was He impure. Why then was He so overwhelmed with desolation? The answer, Luther realized, must be that Christ took on Himself the iniquity, or sins, of us all. He identified Himself so completely with sinful humanity that He felt our alienation from God. He experienced estrangement from the Holy Father.

Paul sums up this idea very neatly: "For He [that is, God the Father] made Him who knew no sin [that is, God the Son] to be sin for us, that we might become the righteousness of God in Him."—2 Corinthians 5:21, NKJV.

For Martin Luther, this was a startling new picture of Christ. In the 1500s, Jesus was always depicted as a solemn judge seated on a rainbow of glory, ready to judge sinners. But here in the Psalms, Luther saw Him as the One who suffers with us.

He saw that God's wrath is always mixed with His mercy—that His judgment can't be separated from His work of reconciliation. Now, there's a very good reason that Luther needed this picture of the merciful Christ. He had spent many years at an Augustinian monastery in Erfurt. It was here that he struggled through those long nights. It was here that darkness engulfed his soul.

He was trying to be perfect, with penance and with prayers, trying somehow to earn God's favor. Luther had always been particularly sensitive, and he often agonized over guilt.

One sultry summer day, Luther was walking back to the town of Erfurt after a visit with his parents in their home of Eisleben.

The sky suddenly turned gray. It began to rain down on that lonely road. It was pouring, with thunder and lightning. The storm broke in all its fury. And suddenly a fierce bolt of lightning struck nearby with such force that it knocked Martin to the ground.

He was terrified. He felt he'd just seen the all-terrible God in this flash of blinding light. So he cried out to his father's patron saint—one whom he believed would help him. He said, "Saint Anne, help me! I'll become a monk."

That fearful promise set the stage for Martin's life.

He fulfilled that vow and began a strictly disciplined life of self-denial and devotion in the Augustinian monastery.

Another crisis experience occurred soon after Luther had become a priest. It was his first day to offer mass in church. Luther took his place at the altar and recited the introductory portion of the ceremony. But something happened when he uttered the words, "We offer unto thee, the living, the true, the eternal God. . . ."

This is how Luther described his feelings: "At those words I was utterly stupefied and terror-stricken. I thought to myself—with what tongue shall I address the Majesty? Who am I that I should lift up mine eyes or raise my hands to the divine Majesty? At his nod the earth trembles. And shall I, a miserable little pygmy, say, 'I want this, I ask for that'? For I am dust and ashes and full of sin and I am speaking to the living, eternal and the true God."

After that experience, Luther redoubled his efforts. Somehow he must become worthy of the holy God— somehow he must earn enough merit to stand before Him.

The trouble was, confessing his sins only made Luther conscious of more sins that needed confessing. And he was obsessed with making sure he remembered every wrong he'd committed. Each one had to be taken care of. After six hours spent in the confessional booth, he could still go out and stop short, remembering something that had eluded his self-analysis.

After one long session, the confessing priest became exasperated. "Look here," he said, "if you expect Christ to forgive you, come in with something to forgive—blasphemy, adultery—instead of these peccadilloes."

Luther exhausted himself trying to be good enough, trying to take care of guilt. He tried all the sacraments, all the means of grace that the church offered. But he could never quite escape the threat of this ominous, holy God overhead. He still felt vulnerable to that bolt of lightning.

That's why he needed a solution so badly. And that's why the picture in Psalm 22, of the Christ who suffers with us, meant so much to him. That's why Romans 3:24 meant so much to him: "Being justified freely by His grace through the redemption that is in Christ Jesus."—NKJV.

This brought joy to his heart. Luther lived in the Augustinian monastery in Wittenberg for thirty-six years. He often spent time in these open cloisters, discussing the Bible with his students. Here, he began to see more and more about grace in the New Testament. He began a detailed examination of the book of Romans. The first thing Luther noticed was the theme of God's justice. This idea was quite frightening to him, as he explained it—and I quote Luther: "I longed to understand Paul's epistle to the Romans. And nothing stood in the way, but that one expression—the justice of God. Because I took it to mean that justice whereby God is just and deals justly in punishing the unjust. My situation was that, although an impeccable monk, I stood before God as a sinner troubled in conscience and I had no confidence that my merit would assuage Him."

But Luther kept studying, and he began to look carefully at the original Greek words behind the Latin text. And he made an important discovery. The theme that dominated the book of Romans wasn't only justice—the strict enforcement of the law. It was justification. Paul emphasized justification by faith.

And Luther knew that justification was a legal word related to a judge suspending a sentence or pardoning a criminal. This meaning came through in passages such as Romans 5:1, 2: "Therefore, having been justified by faith, we have peace with God through our Lord Jesus Christ, through whom also we have access by faith into this grace in which we stand."—NKJV.

Now, listen to Luther describe how all this came together for him as new life and new light. His words illuminate the very moment that transformed his life and that would lead to the transformation of Christendom.

"Night and day I pondered until I saw the connection between the justice of God and the statement that the just shall live by his faith. Then I grasped that the justice of God is that righteousness by which, through grace and sheer mercy, God justifies us through faith. Thereupon I felt myself to be reborn and to have gone through open doors into Paradise. The whole of scripture took on new meaning. This passage of Paul became to me a gate of heaven."

Luther's long, agonizing struggle was over. He had found a way to deal with guilt. He had found a way to ultimate security.

Now, sometimes when we look back at the Protestant Reformation, we see a great deal of theological warfare going on. All kinds of people were engaged in doctrinal battles. And sometimes, all the talk about unmerited grace and legal standing before God and justification and sanctification—these big words—discourages us.

But, I'd like to suggest that what Luther discovered in God's Word is a truth that goes to the very heart of human existence. It relates directly to the most pressing issues people struggle with today.

In rediscovering the gospel, Luther discovered God's solution to the problem that underlies all other human problems—how do sinful human beings form a healthy relationship with a holy God?

True, many people today might not express their most basic need in these terms. Today, we talk about the "problem of insecurity," or the "disease of codependency," or the "issue of guilt feelings." We use a lot of different words and phrases to get to the root of our trouble, the trouble inside of us.

But behind it all is the same problem with which Luther struggled. Human beings fall short of expectations—their own, other people's, and God's. They fall short, yet they desperately need acceptance. They desperately need to feel that they are one with God—that they have an internal peace inside of themselves, that they have worth, that they can live a healthy life.

Listen, friends, you can have all the therapy you want, all the affirmation from other people you want, but if you haven't come to terms with the issue of acceptance with God, you'll never feel truly secure. Luther did everything he could think of on his own in order to be good enough. But it was never enough. He kept falling short.

The book of Romans, however, showed Him a way out, through God's gift of justification by faith. And this is what it boils down to. Paul describes Christ's great act of atonement on the cross in these words: "But now a righteousness from God, apart from law, has been made known. . . . This righteousness from God comes through faith in Jesus Christ to all who believe. There is no difference, for all have sinned and fall short of the glory of God, and are justified freely by his grace through the redemption that came by Christ Jesus. God presented him as a sacrifice . . . so as to be just and the one who justifies those who have faith in Jesus."—Romans 3:21-26, NIV.

People need righteousness before God. THAT'S the solution to our problem of guilt and insecurity. It's not enough to just have people tell us we're OK—especially when we know we're NOT OK. It's not enough to try to sweep our moral failures under the rug. They always come back to haunt us.

What we need is righteousness. We need to be able to stand before a holy God with a clear conscience. That's the only way we can have peace of mind and genuinely feel good about ourselves.

But, humanly speaking, that's impossible, friend. Sinful people can't come up with enough righteousness, no matter how long and hard they try. In fact, the more sensitive someone is, the more and more sinful he or she feels in the struggle they have with sin. Martin Luther wrestled with that dilemma.

So how do we escape our human dilemma? God creates a way out. He makes this thing called righteousness a GIFT. Jesus Christ lived a perfect life as the beloved Son of God. He created this essential righteousness as a man, out of His own blood, sweat, and tears. And then on the cross, He poured that perfect life into us. That's what His shed blood symbolizes— the righteous life of Christ poured out on the cross, on our behalf.

Through the cross of Calvary, righteousness—right standing with God—is a gift. It's a gift that anyone can receive by faith. Everyone has fallen short, but anyone can come to the Cross and receive this incredible gift. Anyone can be justified before a holy God by faith in Jesus Christ.

This is the truth that transformed Martin Luther's life. It's the truth that transforms our relationship with God. Finally, we stand before Him, acknowledging our need, acknowledging our sinfulness, and at the same time, receive His righteousness, His acceptance. When God looks at us, He doesn't see our inadequacy—He sees the perfection of His own Son.

Martin Luther expresses it beautifully. Listen to his words: "If you have a true faith that Christ is your Saviour, then at once you have a gracious God, for faith leads you and opens up God's heart and will to you, that your sinful self is gone. See His pure grace and overflowing love. Thus it is to behold God in faith that you should look upon His fatherly, friendly heart, in which there is no anger nor ungraciousness."

Martin Luther left the Christian world a wonderful legacy. He championed the truth of justification by faith when church tradition had all but stamped it out. He also gave his German contemporaries a translation of the Bible in their own language.

Shortly after church officials condemned Luther's works at the Diet of Worms, his friends decided he needed a hiding place. They feared that he might soon be burned at the stake. So Luther was brought to Wartburg Castle in great secrecy. He accepted his exile from the heat of battle rather reluctantly. His letters from the castle to his friends were penned with the inscription, "From the Wilderness," or "From the Isle of Patmos."

But he decided to use his time in the castle to translate the entire New Testament into German. It was then available only in Latin, which few people could read or understand. Luther's translation was a real breakthrough. It made the gospel clear and understandable for thousands of Germans. And they used it for hundreds of years.

But this man's greatest legacy was his rediscovery of the source of ultimate security for human beings. He raised up the truth of justification by faith like a great banner, and he waved it courageously in the face of tremendous opposition.

That truth still stands over us. It is there to offer us protection and safety. In fact, it's very much like a great castle in which we can find a hiding place from the guilt and insecurity that plague us so much.

While in the castle, Martin Luther looked to the book

of Psalms for his encouragement. He found in Psalm 61:3 a great strength: "For You have been a shelter for me, and a strong tower from the enemy."—NKJV.

Through the sacrifice of Jesus Christ, God has thrown up a great wall around us. He's given us a strong tower.

God says, "I can be just and the Justifier of anyone who has faith in Jesus Christ. I can accept you just as eagerly as I accept My own beloved Son." That's a great castle to be in, friends. It's strong and solid. It's a good home to have.

Let me tell you what happened to a troubled boy named Freddie. Freddie had a serious problem. He just couldn't stop stealing. This pug-nosed ten-year-old with unruly hair kept getting nabbed by the local store owners. His parents were at their wits' end. They'd tried everything to help him break this habit. They'd tried punishment. They'd tried kindness. They'd even tried bribes.

Mom and Dad placed the boy in the hands of a psychologist, then asked for help from "moral welfare" associations. Freddie went on stealing. Nothing seemed to have any effect.

But one day, he met his match. She was an elderly, unmarried lady who'd spent her life in religious work. There wasn't anything about this kindly, unassuming woman to suggest that she could wield any kind of power over a juvenile delinquent. But they said Miss Shaw had a way with kids. So Freddie's parents asked if she might take an interest in the boy.

"Send him over," Miss Shaw said, "I'll do what I can."

A few days later, Freddie reluctantly rang the lady's doorbell. Miss Shaw greeted him cheerfully and said, "Oh! You've just come over at the right moment. I need some change. I wonder if you'd run down to the post office with this $100 bill and get it changed. I'd be most obliged."

Fifteen minutes later, Freddie was back, holding all the change out in the palm of his hand. His face beamed. For the first time, someone really trusted him, someone really believed in him.

And that act proved transforming. Freddie not only gave up petty theft, he became a believer who brought joy back into his home and in time brought many others to Christ.

You know, justification by faith is like that $100 bill. God places this incredible gift of righteousness in our hands. It's the priceless righteousness of His own Son, symbolized by His shed blood. We stare at that gift, and we finally realize how much God loves us—we realize what He's entrusted to us.

That gift proves transforming. In the joy of our acceptance as sons and daughters of God, we want to *live* like sons and daughters of God. We want to be worthy of His trust.

Do you have a rock-solid sense of security in your life right now? Are you living in a walled-up castle, or are you always looking for shelter from guilt and insecurity?

Why not come into God's place of refuge right now? Why not accept God's special hiding place right now? You can be safe in His arms. You can be secure in His declaration, "This is My beloved Son. This is My beloved daughter. I don't see your mistakes anymore. I don't see your faults anymore. I only see the righteousness of My beloved Son."

FIVE

I need hope that death is not the end.

Eyewitnesses of the Unbelievable

THEY WERE THREE SKEPTICS—three people in the depths of depression and despair. They were the most unlikely people to make up some story about a resurrection of their Lord. Yet they were about to have an encounter with the most glorious event in history. They were about to become eyewitnesses of the unbelievable.

Mary, Peter, and Thomas all were surprised by joy. The resurrected Christ burst the bonds of the tomb and appeared to them. Ecstatic, they were fully satisfied.

Mary Magdalene and two friends felt numb as they walked through the streets of Jerusalem to the outskirts of the city. It was very early on a Sunday morning. The sun was just lighting up the eastern sky. The two women stared down at the cobblestones as they clutched burial spices against their garments.

Their beloved Friend Jesus had streaked this pavement with His blood just the day before. He'd stumbled along toward the place of execution with a cross on His torn shoulders. Those horrible scenes were still vivid. The women couldn't get them out of their minds.

The death of Jesus had meant the end of everything for Mary. The end of forgiveness. The end of love. The end of hope. She didn't want to live in a world that could not tolerate a man like this Rabbi from Nazareth.

As they began to walk up a hill toward the place of burial, Mary suddenly stopped. She realized that, in their confusion and gloom, they hadn't thought of one important obstacle. They hadn't thought of the stone.

Mary asked, "Who will roll the stone away from the entrance?" Tombs of the time were sealed with enormous round stones that were very difficult for even strong men to move. The women didn't have a chance of budging one. How were they going to get inside to anoint the body of their Master? He'd been taken down from the cross, broken and limp, and laid in a vault carved out of rock. It hadn't been a proper burial. These women wanted to perform this one last act of devotion.

But the stone stood in their way. They looked at each other. Not knowing what else to do, they walked on toward the tomb. At least they could pay their respects at the site.

Meanwhile, back in the city, a man named Peter huddled in an upper room with the other disciples—the door securely locked, the lamps turned down low.

The hopes of these men had also been crushed by the death of Jesus. Their Master had allowed Himself to be crucified by religious bigots. Where was the kingdom of heaven that He'd spoken so glowingly about? Where was the new era of mercy and justice He'd claimed was beginning? Nowhere, it seemed.

The worst of men had triumphed. The cruelest had claimed the last word. If the Almighty wouldn't protect this spotless Lamb of God, how could they hope to survive? The disciples were sure it was only a matter of time before their enemies burst through the door and put them out of their misery.

Peter was uncharacteristically quiet this morning. He agonized more than anyone else. This disciple carried an additional burden. He couldn't forget the last look he'd seen on Jesus' face. It had happened in the courtyard of the high priest Caiaphas. It happened when Peter denied for the third time that he knew Jesus. He'd betrayed the Man who meant everything to him. And now it was too late to say how sorry he was.

About this same time, one of the disciples, Thomas, was wandering the streets of Jerusalem alone. Thomas was a sensitive, rather melancholy man. The horror of the Crucifixion had affected him deeply. Weeks before, he'd made a resolution. He'd been ready to come to Jerusalem, the city full of Christ's enemies—yes, to come here and die with his Master. He'd said so. But now that Jesus really had been killed, now that He'd been so humiliated in His death, Thomas just wanted to get away. It was too painful to think about. He didn't even want to be around the other disciples, his closest friends. If he looked into their eyes, he'd just remember what they, too, had witnessed—the bloody cross, the spear driven into Jesus' side.

So Thomas wandered alone, with his cloak pulled over his head. Anonymous. Hopeless. Wrapped up in his dark thoughts.

Mary Magdalene. Simon Peter. Thomas. These three were about to meet the One they were mourning—meet Him in a most unexpected way. They were about to become eyewitnesses to the most glorious single event in human history.

Some people today are inclined to dismiss their testimony. It's so fantastic it sounds like the stuff of legend. It sounds like a hallucination.

But listen carefully to their accounts. Scholars who have studied all the evidence surrounding the Resurrection find that it's very hard to break these witnesses down. It's very hard to poke holes in their stories. There is strong evidence, in fact, that they could not possibly have made up the encounter that utterly changed their lives and changed the world.

Mary Magdalene arrived at the tomb on that Sunday morning with her friends, carrying spices to anoint the body of Jesus. But she discovered something very surprising. The historian Luke tells us about it:

"But they found the stone rolled away from the tomb. Then they went in and did not find the body of the Lord Jesus."—Luke 24:2, 3, NKJV.

The huge stone had somehow been moved. But so had the body of their Master. Their first thoughts weren't hopeful ones. They assumed someone had stolen the body. And this made them even sadder. Their beloved Jesus hadn't had a proper burial; now He couldn't even rest in peace. But they were in for more surprises.

"And it happened, as they were greatly perplexed about this, that behold, two men stood by them in shining garments. Then, as they were afraid and bowed their faces to the earth, they said to them, 'Why do you seek the living among the dead? He is not here, but is risen!'"—Luke 24:4-6, NKJV.

Here was wonderful news indeed! Jesus had risen from the dead! But that news just didn't sink in right away. These women had just seen their Lord wrapped in linen—a pale, blue corpse. His body had disappeared, true enough. But a resurrection wasn't the first explanation that came to mind. In fact the account in Mark's gospel tells us this:

"So they went out quickly and fled from the tomb, for they trembled and were amazed. And they said nothing to anyone, for they were afraid."—Mark 16:8, NKJV.

That was their first reaction. They were bewildered, afraid. That's understandable. Resurrections don't happen every day.

But after a bit, these women gathered their wits about them and decided they'd better go and tell the disciples what they'd seen and heard.

So they went to that upper room, knocked on the door, and crept inside. The women had important news: The tomb was empty. But note how the disciples reacted:

"Then they returned from the tomb and told all these

things to the eleven and to all the rest. . . . And their words seemed to them like idle tales, and they did not believe them."—Luke 24:9, 11, NKJV.

This doesn't sound like people about to make up stories, about to start legends. The disciples found the report of a risen Christ incredible. They just couldn't get their minds around it. The empty tomb wasn't enough—not in the beginning. They couldn't switch from despair to hope that easily.

But Peter decided that he'd better at least check it out. So he hurried out the door with John and began running toward the place of burial. John tells us what happened:

"Then Simon Peter came . . . and went into the tomb; and he saw the linen cloths lying there, and the handkerchief that had been around His head."—John 20:6, NKJV.

The burial cloth was there. But there was no Jesus— no body. How did Peter react?

"Bending over, he saw the strips of linen lying by themselves, and he went away, wondering to himself what had happened."—Luke 24:12, NIV.

What had happened? Peter couldn't quite grasp it. The empty tomb, staring him in the face, wasn't enough. It wasn't enough to erase his despair.

But God wasn't finished with His surprises. A bit later Peter experienced something that WAS enough.

"Then, the same day at evening, being the first day of the week, when the doors were shut where the disciples were assembled, for fear of the Jews, Jesus came and stood in their midst, and said to them, 'Peace be with you.' Now when He had said

this, He showed them His hands and His side."
—John 20:19, 20, NKJV.

There He was, standing among them. Peter and his fellow disciples could look into that familiar face. But you know what? They still found it hard to grasp. Luke tells us that they thought, at first, that they were seeing a ghost. It was just too incredible. So this is what Jesus did:

"But while they still did not believe for joy, and marveled, He said to them, 'Have you any food here?' So they gave Him a piece of a broiled fish and some honeycomb. And He took it and ate in their presence."—Luke 24:41-43, NKJV.

Well, this was no pale, broken body. This was no corpse. This was the living Christ—the living Christ having a little supper in their presence. The disciples HAD to believe; they had to accept this incredible fact: Christ really had risen from the dead!

The empty tomb hadn't been enough to overcome their despair. But this latest surprise, this unexpected visit, had erased all their doubts. Jesus had indeed appeared to them, alive and well.

But guess what? That still wasn't enough for one man. One disciple still couldn't bring himself to believe this story.

At some point Thomas came back to that upper room from wandering the streets. He had nowhere else to go, really. And the other disciples met him at the door with breathtaking news. "We have seen the Lord!" How did Thomas respond?

"Unless I see in His hands the print of the nails, and

put my finger into the print of the nails, and put my hand into His side, I will not believe."—John 20:25, NKJV.

The testimony of the other disciples wasn't enough for Thomas. He was so deep into his despair that their word couldn't bring him out of it. Thomas had to see for himself. He had to touch for himself.

Remarkably enough, God wasn't finished with His surprises. John tells us that Jesus met Thomas where he was, still tortured by doubts.

"And after eight days His disciples were again inside, and Thomas with them. Jesus came, the doors being shut, and stood in their midst, and said, 'Peace to you!' Then He said to Thomas, 'Reach your finger here, and look at My hands; and reach your hand here, and put it into My side. Do not be unbelieving, but believing.'"—John 20:26, 27, NKJV.

Thomas touched the wounds in Jesus' side and hands. Thomas saw for himself. And finally, that was enough. Thomas HAD to believe. He had to add his testimony to that of the other disciples.

"Thomas said to him, 'My Lord and my God!'" —John 20:28, NIV.

Friends, this is the right response to the most glorious event in human history. This is the right response to the weight of evidence regarding Jesus' resurrection: "My Lord and my God!"

There is hard evidence that the tomb was empty that Easter morning.

But if that's not enough, there's more. There is clear testimony from eyewitnesses of Jesus appearing alive and well after His death.

And if that's not enough, there's more. There is clear testimony from Christ's closest friends that they touched and saw and heard for themselves. Jesus did indeed rise from the dead. He wasn't a hallucination. He wasn't a ghost. He was there eating a piece of broiled fish in front of their eyes.

My Lord and my God! What else can we say when confronted with the fact of the Resurrection? What other response is appropriate?

I don't think God has held back in giving us evidence of the Resurrection. He hasn't been stingy in giving us proof of Jesus rising from the dead. He's been willing to answer our doubts.

But many times we hold back in responding honestly to this earth-shaking event. Many times we are stingy with our faith, stingy with our hearts.

It can seem like an occurrence far in the distant past. It can seem like old news. It can seem like just another religious doctrine.

But the Resurrection is much more than that. It's the most glorious thing that ever happened on planet Earth. It demonstrates that Jesus can indeed be the Savior of the whole world. It demonstrates that He can be your Savior—that He can be your Savior today. It demonstrates that we can have the hope of eternal life. It demonstrates that the tyranny of sin and death can indeed be broken.

My Lord and my God! We need that kind of response, from the heart, to the fact of the Resurrection. We need that kind of affirmation. We need that kind of worship.

Let me tell you what happened to Mary Magdalene shortly after she looked into that empty tomb on Easter morning. It happened before the message those angels conveyed could really sink in. It happened before she could grasp the fact that her Lord had indeed risen.

Mary had stepped back from the entrance to the tomb and was looking around, probably looking for some sign of where the body of Jesus had been taken. And she spotted a man standing nearby, among the olive trees amid bushes.

This man asked her, "Woman, why are you crying? Who is it you are looking for?" Her response?

"She, supposing Him to be the gardener, said to Him, 'Sir, if You have carried Him away, tell me where You have laid Him, and I will take Him away.'" —John 20:15.

This was Mary's fondest hope at that moment— just to be able to pay her last respects, just to be able to anoint the body of Jesus, just to be able to express one last measure of devotion.

But then the "gardener" called out to her, "Mary." He said her name. And suddenly that day of mourning, that day of sorrow, somersaulted into the first day of a new era—the first day of boundless hope and joy.

It was Jesus who was calling out her name. She knew it. He was standing there with that same wonderful look of love on His face.

Mary rushed toward Jesus and cried out, "Rabboni!" That was what she always called Him—"Teacher."

And Mary fell at the feet of Jesus and clung to Him,

overcome with emotion. She didn't want to lose Him again. She didn't want to ever be apart from her Lord.

But Mary had work to do. She needed to go and tell the disciples the good news. So Jesus gently untangled her arms and told her that soon He would be returning to His Father and her Father, to His God and her God.

How should we respond when the risen Christ appears, when the risen Christ calls us by name? Friends, we'd better come to Him, rush to Him. We need to fall at His feet and worship. We need to cling to the risen Christ.

My Lord and my God! That's the message that rings out from an empty tomb near Jerusalem. It's the message that rings out from Christ's appearances. He appeared in the flesh to over five hundred people after His crucifixion and death. It's the message that rings out from doubting Thomas, the man who touched the wounds of the risen Christ.

Is it the message that's ringing out from your heart today? Is it the good news that gives you hope and assurance today?

I invite you to accept the fact of the Resurrection as the greatest fact in YOUR life. It's about your future. It's about your Savior. I invite you to make the glory of the Resurrection the truth for you.

I invite you this very moment to accept the risen Christ into your heart as Savior and Lord.

SIX

I need to learn how to rest in the
finished work of Jesus for me.

An Advance
on Eternity

THE CASUALTIES on both sides were high.
The shelling was intense. Heavy bombardment from
the artillery lasted all day. The ground shook vio-
lently from the incessant pounding of the Axis-
powers' aircraft. The Allied Forces responded with
a firefight of their own. Ri-
val armies faced each other
across the trenches.

*From the Bible's first book,
Genesis, to its last,
Revelation—from Adam in
Eden to John on Patmos—
believers in all ages have
found satisfying soul rest in
His Sabbath.*

Joe, an eighteen-year-old
American G.I., leaned back
against the earthen wall of his
freshly dug trench, exhausted.
The sun was setting. Another
day had passed, and he was still alive. It was Christmas Eve, 1943. Thoughts of home flooded into his
mind: Mom, Dad, his brother Tom and sister Alice,
freshly baked apple pie, homemade raisin cookies,
roast turkey, colorfully wrapped presents, the Christ-

mas tree, smiles and hugs, logs burning in the fire-
place, hot chocolate . . . and peace.

But in this nightmare called war, death stared him
in the face. "Peace on earth and good will toward men"
were only figments of his imagination.

The battlefield was quiet now. The air was crisp
and clear. The stars twinkled in a moonlit sky. Then he
heard it. Could it really be singing? Were his ears de-
ceiving him this Christmas Eve? Was this some kind
of subtle trap? Was it some sinister plot?

The sounds of a familiar Christmas carol gladdened
the night air. Although the words were German, the
tune was unmistakable:

> *"Silent night, holy night,*
> *All is calm, all is bright.*
> *Round yon virgin,*
> *mother and child . . ."*

In full view a few hundred yards away, German sol-
diers sang Christmas carols. Slowly, cautiously at first,
Joe pulled himself out of his foxhole. His heart was
touched. His emotions were stirred. Suddenly he
couldn't restrain himself any longer. Spontaneously,
he, too, began singing.

> *"Silent night, holy night,*
> *All is calm, all is bright . . ."*

His American colleagues joined in the singing.
Soon voices which a few hours before had shouted
the curses of war echoed a chorus of praise. The
two opposing sides approached each other. They

embraced. They laughed. They sang. For one night, they were brothers. They shared a common humanity. The fighting stopped. The bombing ceased. The mortars were silent.

On that Christmas Eve, for just a brief moment, enemies became friends. In a sense, they recognized a profound truth expressed in Acts 17:24, 26:

"God that made the world and all things therein, seeing that he is Lord of heaven and earth, dwelleth not in temples made with hands. . . . And hath made of one blood all nations of men for to dwell on all the face of the earth, and hath determined the times before appointed, and the bounds of their habitation."—KJV.

The essence of humanity's dignity is a common creation. The fact that we are uniquely created by God places value on every human being. God is our Father. Ours is a shared heritage. We are sons and daughters of the King of the universe. We belong to the same family. We are brothers and sisters fashioned, shaped, molded, by the same God.

Creation provides a true sense of self-worth. The Creator of the universe created me. I am special. When the genes and chromosomes came together to form the unique biological structure of your personality, God threw away the pattern. There is no one else like you in all the universe. You are unique—a one-of-a-kind creation.

Evolution is dehumanizing. If I am an enlarged protein molecule, if I am simply the product of fortuitous chance, if I am only an advanced form of the animal creation, life has little meaning. I am merely one of five billion people clawing at one another for living space on a planet called Earth.

Creation provides a moral imperative for living. I have been created by God, and I am accountable to Him for my actions. The One who made me holds me responsible. He has established absolutes in a world of moral relativism.

Evolution provides no moral ethic for living. Since humans are but advanced animals, it maintains, then, the highest standard is the human mind. Morality is determined from within. There is no absolute, eternal standard to govern behavior.

Creation provides a sense of hope. The God who created me loves me. He cares for me. He will guide me throughout this life.

Evolution looks within to find strength for life's trials. Creation looks without. It looks to a loving, powerful, all-knowing God. Creation provides a sense of destiny.

The God who loves me, who created me, who cares for me, has prepared a place in heaven for me. Death is not a long night without a morning. The grave is not some dark hole in the ground. God has a glorious, new tomorrow planned.

For the evolutionist, death is the end. There is no tomorrow. Creation speaks of hope. Evolution echoes death. Creation speaks of a certain future.

Evolution speaks of blind chance. Creation answers the eternal questions of life. Where did I come from? Why am I here? Where am I going?

Evolution provides a distorted view of life's origin,

fails to address the question of life's purpose, and leaves the soul barren regarding life's ultimate destiny.

Creation unites us with God.

◆ It establishes our self-worth.

◆ It forges our ties with all humanity.

◆ It creates a common ancestry.

◆ It inspires confidence in a God who cares.

◆ It links us to God's inexhaustible power.

◆ It encourages us with the hope of life after death.

It is because our world so desperately needs the reassuring message of Creation that God gave us the Sabbath.

In the mid-1800s, when the evolutionary hypothesis was taking the intellectual world by storm, God sent a message of incredible hope. It is found in Revelation 14:6, 7:

"And I saw another angel fly in the midst of heaven, having the everlasting gospel to preach unto them that dwell on the earth, and to every nation, and kindred, and tongue, and people, Saying with a loud voice, Fear God, and give glory to him; for the hour of his judgment is come: and worship him that made heaven, and earth, and the sea, and the fountains of waters."—KJV.

God's last-day message calls all humanity back to worshiping Him as the Creator of heaven and earth. The basis of all worship is the fact that God created us. Accept evolution, and you destroy the very basis for worship. John the revelator succinctly states it in these words:

"Thou art worthy, O Lord, to receive glory and honour and power: for thou hast created all things, and for thy pleasure they are and were created."—Revelation 4:11, KJV.

He is worthy, precisely because He has created. If God has not created us, if we merely evolved and life is a cosmic accident based on chance and random selection, there is absolutely no reason to worship.

In an age of evolution, God has given the Sabbath as an eternal symbol of His creative power and authority. The Sabbath is a weekly reminder that we are not our own. He created us. Life cannot exist apart from Him. "In him we live, and move, and have our being."—Acts 17:28, KJV.

The Sabbath calls us back to our roots. It's a link to our family of origin. The Sabbath has been observed continuously since time began. It is an unbroken connection back through time to our Creator. The Sabbath tells us that we are not just a product of time plus chance. It keeps us focused on the glorious truth that we are children of God. It calls us to an intimate, close relationship with Him.

When Schia was four years old, her baby brother was born. Little Schia began to ask her parents to leave her alone with the new baby. They worried that like some four year olds, she might be jealous and shake or hit the baby, so they said No.

Over time though, since Schia wasn't showing signs of jealousy, they changed their minds and decided to let Schia have her private conference with "Baby." Elated, Schia went into the baby's room and shut the door, but it opened a crack, enough for her curious parents to peek in and listen. They saw Schia walk quietly up to her baby brother, put her face close to his and say, "Baby, tell me what God feels like. I am starting to forget."

The truth is, we all tend to forget. That's why God says, "Remember." The Sabbath is a weekly reminder of what God is like. It calls us to a new relationship with Him.

In an attempt to destroy the uniqueness of our creation, the devil has introduced a not-so-subtle counterfeit. The counterfeit, which is accepted by even some among us, goes something like this: God is the prime cause of creation, but He took long ages to bring the world into existence. Evolution was the process He used.

This approach attempts to harmonize so-called "scientific data" with the Genesis account. It asserts that the days of creation are long, indefinite periods of time. It accepts the evolutionary viewpoint that the earth is tens of millions of years old. This syncretistic viewpoint creates far more problems than it solves. It completely disregards the psalmist's statement:

"By the word of the Lord the heavens were made, and all the host of them by the breath of His mouth . . . . For He spoke, and it was done; he commanded, and it stood fast."—Psalm 33:6, 9, NKJV.

It overlooks the clear declaration of Hebrews 11:3: "Through faith we understand that the worlds were framed by the word of God, so that things which are seen were not made of things which do appear."—KJV.

The linguistic structure of Genesis 1 and 2 does not permit any other conclusion but that God created the world in six literal days of twenty-four hours and rested the seventh. The Hebrew word for "day" is *yom*. Throughout the Bible, every time a number precedes the word *yom* as an adjective, it limits the time period to twenty-four hours. There is not a single instance in the Bible where a numeral proceeds the noun *yom* and indicates an indefinite period. Without exception, it is always a twenty-four-hour period.

To accept the false idea of long, indefinite periods of creation is to challenge the linguistic structure of Scripture. It is to superimpose personal opinion upon the grammatical structure of God's Word.

Furthermore, if God did not create the world in six literal days, what significance does the seventh-day Sabbath have?

"Remember the Sabbath day, to keep it holy. . . . For in six days the Lord made heaven, and earth, the sea, and all that is in them, and rested the seventh day. Therefore the Lord blessed the Sabbath day and hallowed it."—Exodus 20:8-11, NKJV.

It would make absolutely no sense at all to leave the Sabbath as an eternal legacy of a six-day creation week if a six-day creation week never existed. To accept long ages of creation is to challenge the very need for the seventh-day Sabbath. It is to challenge the authority of the Bible. It is to raise serious questions regarding the integrity of Scripture.

I believe that Satan is challenging the very heart of God's authority by attacking Creation and the Sabbath. The Sabbath is not merely good advice. It is a command from the very throne of God. To lightly disregard the Sabbath, to treat the Sabbath as common, ordinary, or as any other day, is to destroy the essence of our faith relationship with God.

The Sabbath is a holy day, not a holiday. While our own individual choices on Sabbath observance may not always be exactly the same, there is one common principle—the Sabbath has been given to us by a loving Creator to unite us with Him. The heart of the Sabbath is relationship—the acknowledgment that God is worthy of our most supreme devotion, our deepest allegiance, and our total loyalty.

But there is another way that the Sabbath speaks courage to our weary hearts. It shows us that we can rest in Christ for our salvation. The Sabbath is a symbol of rest, not works. It is a meaningful symbol of righteousness by faith, not legalism. It is a clarion call to trust in Jesus and not in ourselves.

The writer of Hebrews uses the Sabbath as an illustration of this rest in Christ. He declares,

"There remains therefore a rest for the people of God. For he who has entered His rest has himself also ceased from his works as God did from His."—Hebrews 4:9, 10, NKJV.

Entering into true Sabbath rest means that we cease trying to create salvation on the basis of our own efforts. God has saved us in Christ. When Jesus voluntarily poured out His life on the cross, He died the death we deserve. He gave His perfect life as a substitute for our sinful life. The Sabbath is not a symbol of legalism. It is rather an eternal reminder that we rest in Him for our salvation.

The Carpenter from Nazareth built a special dwelling in time for us. We can find refuge there. We can be safe there. His work is complete. It is finished. We can know that in Christ we are accepted by our loving heavenly Father. When we rest on the Sabbath, we are resting in His loving care. We are resting in His righteousness.

Sabbath rest is a symbol of a faith experience in Jesus. It is a graphic illustration of our trust in Him. All week, we work, but on the seventh day, we rest. We turn from our works to a total rest in Christ. In Jesus, we have some place to belong. We need not stressfully work out our own salvation. Our lives need not be filled with guilt and fear and anxiety. The Sabbath reveals a restful attitude. Salvation comes only through Jesus. We do not deserve it. We cannot earn it. We rest and receive it by faith.

When Jesus breathed His last and cried, "It is finished," He closed His eyes and died. The work of redemption was complete. He rested on the Sabbath, symbolizing a completed or finished work.

At the end of Creation week, God rested, symbolizing a finished work. Each Sabbath as we rest on the last day of the week, we, too, declare, "God, I am resting in the completed work of Christ on the cross. 'Nothing in my hand I bring. Simply to Thy cross I cling.'"

There is yet another reason God gave us the Sabbath. The prophet Ezekiel declares, "Moreover also I gave them my sabbaths, to be a sign between me and them, that they might know that I am the Lord that sanctify them."—Ezekiel 20:12, KJV.

Here's another reason God gave us the Sabbath. It shows that the Lord is the One who sanctifies us. How is that? Well, that's what God did to the seventh day. It was an ordinary slice of time just like any other at the end of Creation week, but God set this particular day apart. He sanctified it. And through the Sabbath, God tells us, "That's what I want to do for you, too. I want to set you apart as My special child. I want to pour Myself into you. I want to sanctify you. I want to share My holiness with you."

The Sabbath reminds us of where we develop character—in relationship with our heavenly Father and with Jesus Christ. The Sabbath is a continual living promise of God's ability to help us grow through all the ups and downs, the tragedies and triumphs, of our lives. We need that distinctive time with the heavenly Father. We need Sabbath quality time with the God who sanctifies us—the God who helps us keep growing.

The Sabbath has continued in the weekly cycle from the dawn of Creation until now. The Sabbath began in the Garden of Eden, and the Sabbath will be celebrated when this earth is renewed after Christ's second coming. The prophet Isaiah talks about the time when God will make the "new heavens and the new earth." He says:

"'It shall come to pass that from one New Moon to

another, and from one Sabbath to another, all flesh shall come to worship before Me,' says the Lord."—Isaiah 66:23, NKJV.

The Sabbath beautifully represents a forever relationship with God. It stretches from the Garden of Eden at Creation to the garden that God will make of this planet at the end of time. It stretches from paradise lost to paradise restored.

We need that kind of forever in our lives. We need a place that reassures us that we are in an eternal relationship with the heavenly Father. We need a palace in time where that assurance can sink in deep—a place that says our heavenly Father will always be there for us. In the Sabbath, we can find a sense of contented rest. We can get in touch with our roots as His children there. We can grow and mature there. Yes, we need that kind of forever place that ties the whole of our lives to an eternal relationship with God.

Readers Digest wrote of the late Harvey Penick: "For 90-year old golf pro, Harvey Penick, success has come late." His first golf book, *Harvey Penick's Little Red Book,* sold more than a million copies. His publisher, Simon and Schuster, believes the book is one of the biggest selling sports books of all time. The story of the book's publishing is fascinating. Harvey Penick certainly didn't write it for the money.

In the 1920s, Penick bought a red spiral notebook and began jotting down his personal observations regarding golf. He never showed the book to anyone except his son for nearly seventy years. In 1991, he shared it with a local writer and asked the man if he thought it was worth publishing. The writer was elated. He contacted the publishing giant Simon and Schuster immediately. The next evening the publishers agreed to a $90,000 advance.

The jubilant writer passed the news on to Penick's wife. When the writer saw Penick later in the evening, the old man seemed troubled. Something was seriously bothering him. Finally he came clean. With all of his medical bills, there was no way he could advance Simon and Schuster that much money to publish his book. The writer had to explain that Penick would be the one to receive the money.

An advance of $90,000 was his, and he didn't even realize it. In the Sabbath, God has given us an "advance" on eternity. Every Sabbath, heaven touches earth as the Jewish author Abraham Heschel so aptly put it: "The Sabbath is a palace in time." The Sabbath calls us from the things of time to the things of eternity. It calls us to enter into His heavenly rest. It calls us to experience a foretaste of heaven today. It calls us to a relationship with our Creator that will continue throughout eternity. The Sabbath is in actuality an advance on eternity. There is much more coming, but in the Sabbath we have the first installment.

Is it possible that in the busyness of life, Sabbath is a day when we are too exhausted to renew our relationship? Is it possible that in the stress of life, Sabbath is a day of superficial worship rather than intimate fellowship with God? Is it possible God is calling us to something deeper, something broader, something higher, something larger than we have ever experienced before?

Is it possible God longs for us to see a new depth of meaning in the Sabbath? Is it possible that He yearns for us to experience a genuine heart revival this Sabbath? Do you hear Him speaking to your heart today, saying, "Come to Me, all you who labor and are heavy laden, and I will give you rest."?—Matthew 11:28, NKJV.

Why not open your heart to Him right now? Why not plead with Him to satisfy the inner hunger of your soul? Why not ask Him right now to give you a foretaste of eternity this coming Sabbath?

SEVEN

I need to learn how to stand firm,
bow low, and hang on.

Still Standing Tall

A NUMBER OF YEARS AGO, Nikita Khrushchev, premier of the former Soviet Union, gave a major address on the state of Soviet affairs before the Supreme Soviet in Moscow. During his presentation, Khrushchev was highly critical of Stalin. While Khrushchev was speaking, someone from the audience sent up an embarrassing note. "Premier Khrushchev, what were you doing when Stalin committed all these atrocities?"

Daniel lived by the convictions of a conscience conditioned by the principles of God's Word. Even in captivity to Babylon's hostile forces, he discovered a God who would never abandon him—and he was fully satisfied.

Khrushchev angrily shouted, "Who sent up this note?" Not a person stirred.

"I will give him one minute to stand up." The seconds ticked off. Still no one moved.

"All right, I will tell you what I was doing. I was

doing exactly what the writer of this note was doing—exactly nothing! I was afraid to be counted."

Afraid to be counted. Afraid to take a stand. Afraid to stand tall.

It seems to me that if there ever was a time in the history of the world when God has been looking for men and women to take moral stands, to live lives of integrity, to stand tall, it's today.

◆ If you do not stand for something, you will fall for anything.

◆ If you do not stand for something, your faith isn't worth very much.

◆ If you do not stand for something—if there's nothing worth dying for—there is little worth living for.

◆ If there is nothing you are passionate about, if nothing really matters, if everything is a spiritual blur on the radar screen of your mind, life itself will hold little value.

God is calling us to stand tall.

Let's consider now the life of one who stood tall. We shall let his courage and faith speak to us. He is one of history's courageous giants.

◆ He served under at least five heads of state.

◆ He began his diplomatic service shortly after he graduated from high school—and his governmental service continued for approximately over sixty years.

◆ Kings valued his counsel.

◆ Politicians treasured his judgment.

◆ Statesmen sought out his wisdom.

◆ When his nation fell to a foreign power, this valued Secretary of State was amazingly appointed to another term by the foreign conquering power.

Daniel's incredible courage speaks to us of three vital elements of standing tall in a world of moral compromise: standing firm, bowing low, and hanging on.

◆ You cannot stand tall unless you are willing to stand firm.

◆ You cannot stand tall unless you are willing to bow low.

◆ You cannot stand tall unless you are willing to hang on.

Stand Firm

Still in his teens, Daniel was taken captive by the Babylonians, when King Nebuchadnezzar took Jerusalem in 605 B.C. Nebuchadnezzar took a number of Hebrews captives. And some of them, he planned to educate in the principles and policies of Babylon and then send them back as puppet rulers to rule in his stead over Jerusalem.

Subtly, gradually, cunningly, Nebuchadnezzar plotted to change their thinking. His goal was to shift their allegiance from the God of Israel to the gods of Babylon.

Early in his captivity, Daniel was ushered into Babylon's banquet hall to eat from the king's table at a lavish feast thrown in honor of Bel-Marduk, the chief Babylonian god. Evidently the feast was a victory banquet—celebrating the triumph of Babylon over Jerusalem.

The food at the feast had been offered to idols. To eat it would be to accept idolatry and acknowledge the superiority of the Babylonian gods to His God. Also, some of the food was unclean. For Daniel to eat it would be to reject his Hebrew heritage.

Then there was the issue of health. Daniel quickly realized that the rich, unhealthful food would rapidly destroy his health and reduce his physical powers, while also impairing his moral judgment. To eat this food would have been for Daniel a compromise of enormous proportions.

"But Daniel purposed in his heart that he would not defile himself with the portion of the king's delicacies, nor with the wine which he drank; therefore he requested of the chief of the eunuchs that he might not defile himself."—Daniel 1:8, NKJV.

Daniel stood tall because he stood firm. He refused to compromise his integrity to gain the king's favor or avoid his displeasure. You can never stand tall unless you can stand firmly on the side of right.

Fast forward now for thirty-nine years. Daniel's decision was not an isolated instance. It wasn't a once-in-a-lifetime kind of decision. Standing firm was part of his character. It was deeply imbedded within the fabric of his being. It was part of his spiritual life.

Daniel is now in his mid-fifties. King Nebuchadnezzar has a dream—a dream of a great tree that is chopped down. Nebuchadnezzar was confused about the dream and wondered what it meant.

Daniel comes in before the king—the greatest monarch, the most powerful man, of the then-known world. But he does not tell Nebuchadnezzar what he wants to hear. He gives him a message from God. Daniel stands tall, because he stands firm in courageously telling the king that unless he repents, his kingdom is going to be chopped down, just as the tree in his dream. He's going to lose his empire, and he will be sent out to wander around like an animal, insane and eating grass.

"O king, let my advice be acceptable to you; break off your sins by being righteous, and your iniquities by showing mercy to the poor. Perhaps there may be a lengthening of your prosperity."—Daniel 4:27, NKJV.

What courage! What resolute purpose! What decisiveness! What firmness! To look into the eyes of the most powerful man in the world and earnestly call him to repentance.

Fast forward another thirty years. Daniel is now in his late eighties. He is still standing firm. He refuses to compromise.

Evil men have plotted against him. They have laid a trap. They have influenced King Darius to pass a decree that it is unlawful to pray to any other power except the king. This is in direct violation to the first commandment: "Thou shalt have no other gods before me." As an old man, Daniel stands tall, because Daniel stands firm.

"Now when Daniel knew that the writing was signed, he went home. And in his upper room, with his windows open to Jerusalem, he knelt down on his knees three times that day, and prayed."—Daniel 6:10, NKJV. I want to remind you that you can never stand taller than when you are on your knees!

As the result of his singular commitment to God, Daniel was thrown into the lions' den. In the face of death, Daniel stood tall, because Daniel stood firm.

◆ At seventeen, he refused to compromise.

◆ In his mid-fifties, he refused to compromise.

◆ In his eighties, he refused to compromise.

Daniel recognized that compromise is fatal to a vibrant spiritual life.

Author Samuel Johnson wrote, "The chains of habit are generally too small to be felt until they are too strong to be broken."

C.S. Lewis added in his *Screwtape Letters,* "The safest road to hell is the gradual one—the gentle slope, the soft underfoot, without sudden turnings, without milestones, without signposts."

C.S. Lewis is right. It is the daily compromises that gradually erode our faith, that are so destructive to Christian life. Compromise is deadly. You will never stand tall unless you stand firm.

In 1992, I was preparing for a major evangelistic series in Eastern Europe. During our negotiations for the auditorium, the official we were dealing with suggested we pay a $20,000 bribe to secure the auditorium. This was quite common after the demise of communism and the fall of the Berlin wall. The way to get things done was simply to pay a bribe. For us, this was unthinkable. What this official was proposing was very troubling. We wanted to handle the situation sensitively, standing for principle without offending the ex-communist official. We told him we would meet together to discuss our response.

Yes, we wanted the stadium, but as we considered the message we'd be sending by paying this bribe, we concluded that even if we lost the use of the stadium, we had to stand firm to our principles. We decided that if God didn't work to change the man's mind, then we were not going to compromise our own moral integrity. We went to our knees and said, "God, we're putting all of this in Your hands."

We sent a message to the official through an intermediary that we would not pay the bribe. He sent a message back and said, "We have met, and we've decided that whatever you pay, it will be in the contract—nothing on the side."

God worked powerfully to open the door and solve our problem. You can never stand tall, my friends, unless you stand firm!

Recently I received a phone call from a young woman in her twenties. She was making a modest salary working in health care. An employee in her department took another job outside the health-care system. This second young woman tried to recruit her friend for a new job at a salary triple what she was making. The executive interviewing her was deeply impressed with her responses to her questions.

As the interview concluded, she said, "I have only one more question. I am a Seventh-day Adventist, and my day of worship is Saturday. Would I have to work any Saturdays at all?"

"That's really not a problem," he answered. "You'd only need to work four Saturdays a year, representing us at major conventions."

"I'm awfully sorry," she replied, "but I wouldn't be able to do that."

"There's one thing I haven't mentioned to you," the man said, ignoring her answer. "When you sign a contract with us, we also will give you significant stock options."

"You know," she said, "your offer is impressive. I don't mean in any way here to sound 'holier than thou,' but I can't work even one Sabbath a year, because to do that would be for me to put money before God. And that's a decision I can't and won't make. But if you can arrange it somehow for me not to work any Sabbaths, then I'd definitely want to work for you."

The word came back. She could not have all her Sabbaths off.

This young woman knew what it is to stand firm. She knew what it is not to compromise. She preferred living on a far lesser salary, yet being at peace, to accepting huge financial rewards simply by compromising her convictions. She would not sell out cheap.

People who stand tall are not blown away by every wind of compromise that comes along. The winds of compromise do not blow them over because they, like Daniel, have "purposed in their hearts" to serve God. They have settled it—obedience matters.

Bow Low

Now, you also can never stand tall unless you bow low. The strength to stand tall is not some mental toughness. It is not some human determination. It is not some extraordinary will power. It is strength of character rooted in a relationship with God through prayer.

Daniel had it. He stood tall because he bowed low. At each crossroad in his life we see him bowing low.

In his youth, when confronted with the threat of death, we see Daniel "seek mercies from the God of heaven concerning this secret, so that Daniel and his companions might not perish with the rest of the wise men of Babylon."—Daniel 2:18, NKJV.

Later in life, when faced with the lions' den, Daniel is found "as his custom" was, the Bible says (Daniel 6:10), praying three times a day with his windows open.

Still later, under a new king, Darius, Daniel is found praying that God will deliver his people from captivity. "Then I set my face toward the Lord God to make request by prayer and supplications, with fasting, sackcloth, and ashes. And I prayed to the Lord my God, . . . and said, 'O Lord, great and awesome God."—Daniel 9:3, 4., NKJV.

Daniel's life was saturated with prayer. He bowed low so he could stand tall.

I have read that when mountain climbers reach the summit of some of the world's greatest peaks, like Mount Everest or Mount McKinley, if the winds are fierce, the only way to keep from getting blown away is to get on their knees on the top. If you want to stand tall on the mountaintop with God, you must bow low.

◆ Daniel prayed to the God of heaven as a youth carried into exile.

◆ Daniel prayed to the God of heaven when presented with the king's delicacies.

◆ Daniel prayed to the God of heaven when thrown into the lions' den.

◆ Daniel prayed to the God of heaven when empires collapsed and kingdoms crumbled.

Daniel stood tall, because Daniel bowed low.

As I've traveled from country to country, I've met some real giants of prayer—men and women who stood tall as did Daniel, because they bowed low.

In Madras, India, Samual Schadrak was my translator who stood by my side. He was unusually fluent and seemed to grasp my every word. He translated with pathos and power in his voice. We were as one team, and when calls were made at the end of the presentations, hundreds came forward to the altar.

One day I talked with Samuel and said, "Pastor Schadrak, tell me a little about your prayer life."

"Oh, Pastor Finley," he replied. "For forty days I fasted before these meetings."

"Did you eat anything at all?" I asked.

"In the middle of the day, just a little chapatti," he replied, "because I wanted my heart clean before God." He told me that through prayer, he had seen miracles:

◆ Evil spirits cast out of demon-possessed men and women.

◆ Hindu hearts converted.

◆ Poverty-stricken, uneducated lay people who became courageous.

◆ Illiterate village people who became warriors for Christ.

Before the Madras presentations, *It Is Written* had hired about 130 Bible instructors to help prepare for the meetings. They met every day to pray.

I remember so well one of our Indian Bible workers— an elderly woman with long, graying hair and a sun-baked face with deeply etched lines. She had a wonderful smile, but her teeth were not in good condition—some teeth were missing. She wasn't well-educated, though she knew God's Word.

And when the Bible workers divided up the city, she asked to be assigned to the worst area of town— a barrio known for its gangs, thieves, drugs, and drinking.

Now, this woman was a true prayer warrior who prayed hours each day. As she visited the area, she would meet with various gang leaders. One day, she was meeting with the leading gang leader of the barrio—a tough, ruthless, blood-thirsty thief and drug addict. He confronted her and said, "Old woman, get out of here with your Jesus."

"Young man," she replied, "tell me why you don't love Him as I do?"

For two hours then, the gang leader ranted and cursed and railed against her and her Jesus. She listened to all he had to say, then said to him, "Young man, I have listened to you for two hours. Now sit down and listen to an old woman."

And he did! She told him about the Jesus she loved, and how He had changed her life. She told him about how Jesus had forgiven her. And she told him the love Jesus had for him—and the love He had put in her heart for him as well. She told him how she had pled in prayer that God would lead her to the leader of the barrio, and that He had answered her prayer. "Even your shouting at me," she told him, "is part of that answer."

Then that tough, hardened gang leader began to weep. "Old woman, please—please come with me to talk to all the other gang leaders and tell them, too, about this Jesus!"

You can never stand firm until you bow low. What is your prayer life like, my friend? Are you bowing low day by day before God? Is "standing firm" for you some kind of do-it-yourself, grit-your-teeth, clench-your-fist kind of standing tall? Or is it a humble relationship with God that leads you to seek His approval more than anything else in life—that leads you to represent Him in everything you do? This bowing-low humility leads you to never compromise your integrity, because if you did, you'd dishonor the God who loves you so much.

Hang On

You can never stand tall unless you stand firm.
You can never stand tall unless you bow low.
And you can never stand tall unless you hang on.
Daniel hung on—he persevered. Daniel never gave up in the tough times.

Daniel did not hang on to *something*. He hung on to *Someone*.

◆ A captive in a foreign land, Daniel hung on to God.

◆ Separated from home and family, Daniel hung on.

◆ In the midst of a heathen culture, Daniel hung on.

◆ In a sex-centered, thrill-jaded, morally twisted, spiritually dwarfed and corrupt society, Daniel hung on.

◆ With his life on the line, Daniel hung on.

◆ Betrayed by working associates, lied about, ridiculed, in the midst of jealousy and envy, Daniel hung on.

◆ Facing his greatest test in his old age, Daniel hung on.

There's a story about an old woman who was

dying of cancer. Over her life, she had memorized hundreds of Bible texts. And one of her favorites was this one:

"I know whom I have believed and am persuaded that He is able to keep what I have committed to Him until that Day."—2 Timothy 1:12, NKJV.

This woman's life was ebbing away. Her strength was gone. Her energy was spent. Her mind was not as clear as before. She could hardly remember a thing. She had repeated this verse over and over throughout the months of her illness. And as her sickness progressed, her mind became increasingly clouded, until she could only remember one phrase: "He is able to keep what I have committed to Him."

Her memory failed further, and on the day before her death, she could only remember three words: "Committed to Him."

On her deathbed, the entire passage faded from memory except one word—"Him." She kept repeating it over and over. She was hanging on to Him, clinging to Him.

And that's enough. Hang on to Him! Jesus Christ is enough! When you have nothing left but Him, you find that He is enough!

Throughout his life, Daniel stood tall because he stood firm. He would not compromise his integrity.

◆ He stood tall because he bowed low. He realized his spiritual strength came from the God of heaven.

◆ He stood tall, because in all circumstances of life

he hung on to Him. Every time we see him in the book of Daniel, he is still standing.

◆ At the king's banquet in Daniel, chapter 1, he is still standing.

◆ At the University of Babylon in chapter 2, he is still standing.

◆ In Belshazzar's banquet hall in chapter 5, he is still standing.

◆ Faced with the threat of the lions' den in chapter 6, he is still standing.

◆ Kingdoms rise and fall, but Daniel is still standing.

◆ Babylon gives way to Media-Persia, and Daniel is still standing.

◆ Kings ascend and descend their thrones: Nebuchadnezzar, Belshazzar, Cyrus, Darius— but Daniel succeeds them all. He is still standing.

◆ Empires collapse, decades pass, kings die. But Daniel is still standing.

And friend, if in these end times, you stand firm, bow low, and hang on, you, too, will be found still standing tall!

EIGHT

*I need more kindness toward
those in my family.*

A Family
Against the Odds

IT USED TO BE EASIER, they say. Raising a family. Times were slower. Life had a friendlier rhythm to it. Neighbors helped. The church bound communities together. Everyone knew and respected the neighborhood policeman. Kids had good, clean room to grow in.

The story of Ruth reveals that relationships really matter. Commitment to her Lord meant commitment to her family. Faithful to God and loyal to her loved ones, Ruth was fully satisfied.

But the world's much different now. The odds are stacked against the family, people say. Life pulls and pushes—relationships tear apart. Drugs and pornography assault our young.

The pressures, the pace, the problems—so much seems stacked against our families today. Can we ever beat the odds?

Earlier in this century, William Phelps could say, "The highest happiness on earth is marriage." But more recently a newspaperman observed, "The three stages of the modern family are: matrimony, acrimony, and alimony."

The odds do seem stacked against families today. But I want to share with you a true story of one family who succeeded against the odds. And this family shows us, in remarkable ways, qualities that are essential in building healthy families today.

The story is found in Ruth, a literary gem tucked away in the Old Testament, right after the book of Judges. It begins with three widows walking down the long road from Moab to Judah. They are Naomi, and her daughters-in-law, Ruth and Orpah. Not much of a family, you might say.

Naomi, a Hebrew woman, is returning to Judah after a long absence. Ten years before, a famine forced her and her family to settle in the country of Moab. She had come with her husband, Elimelech, and two sons. The two young men eventually married Ruth and Orpah—Moabite women.

But then, one by one, all three men died. We don't know how. The book of Ruth simply pictures three sorrowing widows—Ruth and Orpah, left without children, and Naomi, grieving over a devastated family.

Naomi had heard that food was now plentiful in Judah. So she decided to return. And Ruth and Orpah set out on the journey with her, headed toward a foreign land.

But as Naomi walks on this dusty road back to Judah, she stops in her tracks. She begins to think. Ruth and

Orpah will never be able to marry in Judah. As foreigners, they never will be fully accepted. The girls would be far better off staying in Moab. At least among their own people they'd have a chance of raising a family.

So Naomi stops and tells her daughters-in-law: "Go back, each of you, to your mother's home. May the Lord show kindness to you."—Ruth 1:8, NIV.

But Ruth and Orpah promise to go back with Naomi to her people. After all, they're all the elderly woman has left. How could she survive alone?

Naomi, however, insists: "Return home, my daughters. Why would you come with me? Am I going to have any more sons, who could become your husbands?"—Ruth 1:11, NIV.

Naomi really cares about these two girls. She's more concerned about their welfare than about her own security in old age.

You know it's pretty difficult to let go of those we've learned to depend upon. But in old age, it's doubly hard. Supports are falling away. There's a strong urge to hang on tight and cling to every bit of security we have.

But Naomi is able to let go. She shows us a priceless quality—unselfish concern.

So finally, Orpah embraces her mother-in-law tearfully, pulls her close, and says farewell. But Ruth can't tear herself away. Her devotion is too strong. This young girl makes a memorable promise to Naomi. She says: "Where you go I will go, and where you stay I will stay. Your people will be my people and your God my God. Where you die I will die."—Ruth 1:16, 17, NIV.

What a beautiful assurance! What beautiful words! Can you imagine a more eloquent loyalty than that? Forgetting her own hopes for the future, Ruth casts in her lot with her aging mother-in-law. Uppermost in Ruth's thoughts is simply this—she needs me.

The apostle Paul once told his Corinthian converts: "You are in our hearts, to die together and to live together."—2 Corinthians 7:3, NKJV.

Ruth had that same selfless devotion. She shows a remarkable loyalty. That's something we see too little of these days. We live in an age of "disposable relationships." People find it easy to break bonds. If someone is useful to us, or attractive at the moment, fine. If not, we travel on to greener pastures. We're losing that sense of concern for others, of sticking by a friend, no matter what.

What a contrast Ruth provides. She held fast—she clung to that one family bond that remained. It wasn't much, from our point of view—just a widowed old woman. But Ruth turned her back on everything else, for Naomi's sake.

So in our story, Naomi realizes that Ruth is determined to go with her. And the two travel together toward Judah. They must have been happy in the deep concern they shared for each other.

We see so many odds stacked against the family today. The immorality, the career stresses. There's no time for roots to sink in. But imagine for a moment the forces that could have torn Ruth and Naomi apart. That little fragment of a family had a lot going against it.

There was race. Naomi was a Hebrew; Ruth a Moabitess. Their respective peoples had been enemies for centuries. Hebrews considered Moabites to be unclean heathen.

And age difference. We might wonder, how could young Ruth spend the rest of her life with a sorrowful old woman?

Death, too, had come into their lives in force. That's never easy to adjust to. Tragedy has broken apart some of the strongest families.

There was poverty. In that culture, widows had a hard time just surviving. No one had ever heard of life insurance or social security.

And don't forget, Ruth and Naomi were in-laws. How many in-laws do you know who enjoy perfect harmony?

All these factors conspired against the two women. Yet Ruth and Naomi clung together. Ruth gives us one of the most inspiring examples of loyalty in the Bible—"Where you go, I will go."

You know, God is a lot like that. His loving kindness and devotion are often celebrated in the Psalms. One of the words most frequently used to describe Jehovah in the Old Testament is *faithful*. To Israel, God was, first and last, faithful. He could be depended on. He entered into a covenant with His people. His promises were true. Faithful. That's God.

And that was Naomi's religion. She believed in a faithful God. I think her faith must have rubbed off on

Ruth. You remember that Ruth said, "Your God will be my God."

I believe that's one reason why Ruth could give us such a beautiful picture of loyalty. She was responding to the loyalty and faithfulness of Israel's God—a God wholeheartedly committed to His people.

Our families desperately need this kind of faithfulness today—this unconditional loyalty. It all boils down to this: one person committed to another. That's the basic building block of the family.

And God is the greatest source of the loyalty we need. God is faithful. That's what Ruth discovered. She was to discover even more after arriving in Judah.

Naomi led her daughter-in-law back to Bethlehem, the town she'd left ten years earlier. As the village folk crowded around to welcome home their old friend, they stopped for a moment, surprised.

"Can this be Naomi?" they asked one another. "She looks so different, so downcast. Is this the same vibrant, young woman who left Judah with a husband and two fine sons?"

Naomi answered their questioning gazes. "Don't call me Naomi," (which means pleasant) she told her friends. "Call me Mara" (which means bitter). "The Lord afflicted me."

Naomi then told the sad story of what had happened to her family. Only Ruth the Moabitess is left.

In the loss of her loved ones, Naomi's zest for life has been crushed. She's a spiritually defeated woman.

But Ruth realizes that life must go on, even when its taste is bitter. The first thing the two widows need to find is some means of support. They are poor now, without any land to farm. Ruth determines to do something to keep this fragment of a family going.

It would have been easy for her to slip into hopeless apathy. She's just a vulnerable young woman—a foreigner among Hebrews. If her Hebrew mother-in-law can do nothing, what chance does she have? But Ruth refuses to give in to discouragement.

About that time in Judah, the barley harvest was beginning. Everywhere in the countryside around Bethlehem, men were cutting and stacking tall stalks of barley.

Ruth got an idea. She tells Naomi: "Let me go to the fields and pick up the leftover grain behind anyone in whose eyes I find favor."—Ruth 2:2, NIV.

Hebrew law contained a special provision for the poor that applied during harvest time. They were allowed to gather whatever sheaves of grain the harvesters left behind. It was called gleaning. And farmers were to leave corners and edges of their fields uncut so the destitute might have a source of food. The God of Israel had special concern for the poor. He often promised to bless those who were generous to them.

So Ruth set out alone with her grain sack, looking for fields where she could glean. It certainly was not easy work—bending over rows of cut barley, all day, under a hot sun. And it wasn't altogether safe for a poor young woman to work alone among the male laborers.

Ruth had been part of a prosperous family. Now she was forced to gather up the scraps others left behind. Pride might have prevented her from doing that kind of common labor. But Ruth had something stronger going for her: loyalty, commitment. And she faithfully stuck by the task at hand. Day after day, she worked steadily in the fields. And each evening, happily, she brought her gleanings home to Naomi.

Economic hardship stacked the odds against Ruth and Naomi. But Ruth met the challenge. Her loyalty pushed her into action. She cared enough to get involved. She had the kind of love that's willing to get its hands dirty.

A dutiful son of a widowed mother once told his friends, "I love my mother with all my strength."

"How's that?" they asked.

"Well, we live on the top floor of our tenement apartment, four flights up, with no elevator. Mother is busy, and I carry up the coal in a scuttle. And I tell you, it takes all my strength to do it!"

You know, friends, too many families don't exert that kind of strength. Too many families drift apart. Problems come, adversity threatens, and they don't put up a fight.

Sometimes we just complain. We dwell on the problem and reinforce our discouragement. We criticize others for their part in the problem. You know, it's possible to nag one another into inaction. At times we simply withdraw. The problem is someone else's responsibility. We build a cocoon around ourselves and try to shut it all out.

It's easy to do nothing. As one bumper sticker read:

"There's too much apathy!" And in small letters below, "But who cares?" Apathy destroys families. Successful families don't just happen automatically. They require hard work.

You know the saying: "When the going gets tough, the tough get going." Well, Ruth got going. She seized the initiative.

The Bible tells us of others who did the same. Like Joseph. He was betrayed by his own brothers and unjustly imprisoned. But he didn't give in to despair. He became a trusted servant of the jailkeeper and eventually rose to rule with Pharaoh. Loyalty prevailed.

Daniel got going. This devout Hebrew youth was exiled to pagan Babylon. But he didn't give up or give in. He demonstrated God's better way of life to his heathen rulers and became a counselor to kings.

Friends, always remember that God got involved, very much involved with the human family and its problems. It would have been much easier for God to stay out of the sinful mess of our planet. But God came here as a man and labored humbly as a carpenter. He cared enough to get His hands dirty. And God showed us His divine character in the simple everyday duties of life.

God cared for Ruth the Moabitess too. He was gracious to her through a man named Boaz. Ruth found herself working in his field one day. The man noticed how faithfully she labored and asked about her. Boaz found that she was a widow from Moab. Impressed by her diligence, this godly man became Ruth's protector. He made sure she had plenty of grain to take home every day. At mealtime Boaz invited the girl to eat from his provisions.

Soon this man's kindness turned into love. And Ruth found the husband she thought that she could never have as an alien in Judah. This young girl, so loyal and faithful, inspired the faithful devotion of Boaz. Ruth would have a family again. Naomi would get to hold her grandchildren on her lap.

You know, Ruth's effort out in the fields, picking up leftover sheaves, might seem pretty frail. But God blessed her work. This girl had come from Moab to find shelter under the wings of the God of Israel. And He multiplied her gleanings. He showed Himself the same generous God who would later supply the bread and fish and multiply them for the five thousand in Galilee.

Sometimes our efforts seem pretty small and frail. So many forces today tear families apart. The odds seem stacked against us. We feel we just don't have the resources to meet the great problems that burden us.

But remember, God is eager to multiply our efforts. As we act in faith, He responds and magnifies those actions. We can link our weakness to His power. God's resources are inexhaustible.

The important thing is that we ACT, in faith. We must put our loyalty into action. We must fight apathy—take that first step. We must demonstrate a selfless concern that's willing to work for the good of others.

Christian author Corrie ten Boom describes a beautiful person who acted out her selfless concern—her very own mother. Mrs. ten Boom was the kind of person who lived to serve. Her hands were always busy knitting sweaters for orphans, baking bread for the homeless, making birthday gifts. This woman was known and loved by people throughout her Dutch town of Haarlem.

But then a massive stroke left Mrs. ten Boom partially paralyzed. She could only utter three words: "yes," "no," and "Corrie." It appeared that her deeds of love had come to an end.

This seemingly helpless woman, however, soon found a way to care. Every morning the ten Boom daughters set their mother in a comfortable chair by the front window so she could watch the busy street outside. And she began to communicate. They developed a system, something like "twenty questions."

Mrs. ten Boom would call from the window, "Corrie?"

"What is it, Mama?" Her daughter would answer. "Are you thinking of someone?"

"Yes."

"Someone in the family? Somebody you saw on the street?"

"Yes."

"Was it an old friend?"

"Yes."

The daughters called out names until they heard Mama's delighted "Yes!" She'd spotted a childhood friend. And they realized, "Of course, it's her friend's birthday."

Then Corrie would write a note saying that Mama wanted to wish the person a happy birthday. At the close of the note, she helped Mrs. ten Boom's stiff fingers sign her name.

For the last three years of her life, this woman sat at her window and continued ministering to the people outside. Not even paralysis could stop her service of love.

Friends, that kind of selfless concern can make all the difference in our own families. It's not the loud warnings about evil that best protect our families. No, it's the quiet acts of kindness that make family bonds strong. It's not fighting *against* the dangers of the world that count as much as living *for* each other.

Acting out our loyalty, in faith, can beat all the odds—all the forces arrayed against us. If we just take the first steps of *showing* our concern. God will magnify the effort. He'll bless our families abundantly—as abundantly as He blessed that impoverished widow named Ruth, setting off by faith toward a strange land.

Do you sense God calling you to kindness in your own family? Have other priorities entered into your life? God is calling you to loyalty to your wife, to your husband, to your son, to your daughter.

God is calling you to turn your heart toward home.

NINE

I need to be more hopeful and optimistic
about the future.

The Best Is
Yet to Come

MARTHA HAD BEEN A deaconess in her local congregation for over forty years. She was one of those cheerful, optimistic, and truly happy women—a bubbly, smiling deaconess who warmly greeted people as they came into the church. She made sure that they felt welcomed. One hot, sultry summer afternoon, she called Pastor Jim. It was unusual that she would disturb her preacher in the middle of the day.

Moses looked beyond the present to the eternal. Through the eyes of faith, he saw the God whose best was yet to come—and he was fully satisfied.

Martha's voice was troubled. "Pastor Jim, I really need to talk to you. I need to talk to you quickly. Can you come over?"

Jim didn't know quite what was up. It was strange that Martha would call him at that time, but because it was Martha, he dropped what he was doing, rearranged his scheduled priorities, and drove to Martha's house. When he got there, he knew something was wrong.

107

Martha was more anxious than he had thought. They spent a little time talking about the weather. They talked a little bit about Martha's children and grandchildren. They talked a little bit about Jim's family, and then Martha said, "Pastor Jim, this morning I went for my annual checkup. I discovered that I have a malignancy. The malignancy has spread. The doctor gives me at most two months to live. So Pastor Jim, I wanted to talk to you about my funeral. Pastor, here are the hymns that I would like sung:

> *"'Precious Lord, take my hand.*
> *Lead me on; help me stand.*
> *Through the storm, through the night,*
> *Lead me on to the light. . .'*

"Pastor Jim, when I die, I do want the precious Lord. And Pastor, I also love that old hymn,

> *"'What a friend we have in Jesus.*
> *All our sins and griefs to bear.*
> *What a privilege to carry*
> *Everything to God in prayer.'*

"Pastor Jim, here's my favorite text: 'The Lord himself shall descend from heaven with a shout, with the voice of the archangel, and with the trump of God: and the dead in Christ shall rise first: Then we which are alive and remain shall be caught up together with them in the clouds, to meet the Lord in the air' [1 Thessalonians 4:16, 17, KJV]. Pastor

Jim, that's my text. Read it and preach on it at my funeral.

"And Pastor Jim, I want you to come into my bedroom, to my closet, because here is my blue church dress. You know, Pastor, I've worn this dress to church for a number of years now. It wouldn't be church without my old blue dress. Pastor, when they put me in the coffin, I want to buried in that blue dress.

" And Pastor Jim, here's my Bible, and I want you to put my Bible in my left hand—the hand nearest my heart. This Book has encouraged me through the years. So Pastor Jim, when people come by me after the service, I want the coffin opened, and I want them to see old Martha lying in the coffin with a little smile on her face, with her Bible in her hand, and wearing her blue Sabbath dress.

"Oh, and Pastor Jim, there's one more thing. Put a fork in my right hand."

"Martha, I didn't quite get it. Your blue church dress, your Bible, but Martha, why the fork in your right hand? What does that fork mean, Martha?"

"You know, Pastor Jim, I'm a deaconess, and I've been serving at fellowship dinners in this church for the last forty years. And you know that when the fellowship dinner is over, we deaconesses often say 'save your fork.' Now Pastor, when we say 'save your fork,' that's not for some lukewarm, melting vanilla ice cream. That's not for some imitation chocolate pudding from a box.

"When we say 'save your fork,' that means that the best is yet to come! That means the homemade apple pies are coming. That means the homemade blueberry pies are coming. That means the homemade oatmeal raisin cookies are coming. Save your fork—the best is yet to come. So Pastor Jim, when I die, and they put me in the coffin and then go by and look at that fork, they are going to ask, 'What does it mean?' And you are going to tell them, Pastor: 'Martha believed that the best is yet to come!"

◆ If you are on top of the world today—if you are finding fulfillment in your job, your family is fine, your health is good, your finances are doing well—the best is yet to come.

◆ If you are going through discouragement today because your kids, who were brought up in Sabbath School and church, are not attending now, the best is yet to come.

◆ If you're going through the heart-wrenching agony and trauma of divorce, and you are wondering how to pick up the pieces of your life, the best with Jesus is yet to come.

◆ If your body is racked with rheumatism and arthritis, or, for some, the cancer has metastasized, the best is yet to come.

◆ If you come from a broken past and a dysfunctional family, and you are still healing from the scars, the best is yet to come.

◆ If you've been through financial reverses, the best is yet to come.

◆ If you're struggling with guilt, the best is yet to come.

◆ If some sin has gripped and imprisoned you, the best is yet to come.

Let's study the life of Moses, because the life of the follower of God is a life of uninterrupted victories that may not seem to be so here, but will appear to be so in the hereafter.

Moses was cursed at his birth—but God turns curses into blessings.

"And Pharaoh charged all his people, saying, Every son that is born ye shall cast into the river, and every daughter ye shall save alive."—Exodus 1:22, K.JV.

Pharaoh issued that decree concerning the Hebrews, and when he did, he said that every male child should be killed—cast into the river. Pharaoh was concerned because of the spread and growth of the Israelites. So he condemned the Hebrew children to death. Amazingly enough, God turned that curse into a blessing. And with God, our greatest curses are turned at times into our greatest blessings.

The decree's effect was the opposite of what Pharaoh had thought it would be. Follow the biblical line of reasoning. Pharaoh wanted to hold the Israelites in a viselike grip. He wanted to destroy them and keep them from growing, because he was afraid that some leader of the Israelites would rise to prominence and overthrow Pharaoh and the Egyptian forces. So Pharaoh passed a decree that male Hebrew children be put to death.

But as the result of that decree, Moses' mother took him and put him in a little basket, and it was there that through the providence of God, Pharaoh's daughter discovered Moses. And it was because of that decree that Moses received the education in Egypt that enabled him to develop military and leadership skills and gain vast knowledge of geography and history. God could then sanctify and refine and use Moses to lead the Israelites when they were wandering in the wilderness.

The point is that the curse was turned into a blessing. The point is that Pharaoh's intent to destroy Moses became the very vehicle God used to train and educate Moses. It was through that decree that God opened a door for Moses to obtain an education in the courts of Egypt. Praise His holy name, God turns curses into blessings! For with God, the best is always yet to come!

Our life's traumas and heartaches and sorrows are really an uninterrupted series of victories. We may not see them as such here, but in eternity, we will.

◆ Do you come from a broken home? The best is yet to come.

◆ Have you been abused in childhood? The best is yet to come.

◆ Have you gone through the trauma of divorce? The best is yet to come.

Your scars will be stars to shine forever in the kingdom of God.

If God can take the wicked, despicable activities of Joseph's brothers—who threw him into a pit—and take Joseph from the pit to the palace, God can take the activities of others against you, and you can go from the darkness of the pit to the glories of the palace—for the best is yet to come.

If God can take the attack of Nebuchadnezzer on Jerusalem, that gleaming city . . . if God can take the captivity of Daniel, leaving his home, his father, his mother and all his boyhood dreams . . . and if God can use all of that to put Daniel on the throne of Babylon, then the best, for you, is yet to come.

If God can take Paul's imprisonment and use it to write Galatians, Ephesians, Philippians, and Colossians —the great prison epistles—to bless the world, then God can write an epistle in your life through the prison experience you have been through, for the best is yet to come.

If God can take an old rugged cross and a Man with nails through His hands and blood running down His wrists—if God can take a crown of thorns, if God can take a spear, if God can take rusty nails, if God can take the death and agony of the Cross and turn it into an instrument of salvation, even for you, through the Cross—then the best is yet to come.

◆ Look beyond your tears.

◆ Look beyond your sorrow.

◆ Look beyond your heartache.

◆ Look beyond your disappointment.

◆ Look beyond the divorce.

◆ Look beyond the malignancy.

◆ Look beyond the pain.

◆ Look beyond the suffering.

◆ Look beyond the scars, because seeing Him who is invisible, the best is yet to come.

Because He takes our curses and turns them into blessings, as He did for Moses. With Him, the best is yet to come!

Moses was forced to flee—but wilderness wanderings become divine encounters.

After forty years in the schools of Egypt, Moses was forced to flee. You see, there were still some lessons that God was teaching Moses. It was like that bumper sticker I see occasionally: "Have patience with me . . . God isn't finished with me yet." Moses believed he was ready, but God said No, you're not ready.

You see, at the beginning of the forty years of wilderness wandering, Moses said, "Lord, step aside. I'm ready." God said, "Moses, you're not ready." At the end of the forty years, Moses said, "I'm not ready" and God said, "You are ready."

The way we think and the way God thinks are very different sometimes. Moses saw an Egyptian persecuting, whipping, beating, then killing a fellow Hebrew. And in fury, Moses killed that Egyptian. The next day Moses saw two Hebrews arguing, and they said, "Moses, what are you going to do—kill us like you did the Egyptian?"

Moses was forced to flee, because he knew the death penalty was hanging over his head. And he went out into the wilderness—the wilderness of wandering. Dark and alone, discouraged and disappointed. Moses' error was a fatal mistake. He took God's work into his own hands. His objectives were good; his methods were poor.

Now imagine what must have been on Moses' mind in the wilderness wanderings. Discouraged, disappointed. He thought to himself, *God can no longer use me.* Filled with guilt, shame, a sense of failure and defeat, he said, "I have sinned. These are bloody hands. With these hands, I've killed a man. God had dreams for my life, but through my conscious choice, I've spoiled those dreams. God had plans for my life, but I have ruined those plans."

Do you know what I'm talking about? Do you know the feelings of Moses? God had plans for me, but my marriage fell apart. So you say, those plans are gone. My life went in a different direction than I thought it would go. God had plans for me, but I ruined it with alcohol and tobacco. God had plans for me. But although I come to church, I'm unfaithful in my tithe. I break the Sabbath. God had plans for me, but inside I feel shame. I feel guilt because I don't live up to God's ideal. For all of us, there are failures.

For all of us who have not reached God's ideal, consider Moses. Filled with shame, filled with sin, filled with guilt, he kept running, running, running. We do too. We keep our lives filled with frantic activity. We run too. And here, not only does God turn curses into blessings, He turns wilderness wanderings into divine encounters.

"The Lord saw that Moses turned aside to see the bush that was burning."—See Exodus 3:4.

God turned a poor decision into a divine encounter! You know it's quite an incredible thing when you think about it. Why would the Lord have a bush burned but not consumed? Because, a burning bush that is not consumed gets your attention.

And Moses, wandering in the wilderness, running, came face to face with a divine encounter. And God said to him, "Here I am. Draw not near hither. Put off your shoes, for the place where you stand is holy ground."

◆ Holy ground in the wilderness.

◆ Holy ground when I'm running from God.

◆ Holy ground in my disappointment.

◆ Holy ground when I have taken my life into my own hands and made a poor decision.

◆ Holy ground when my plans have failed.

◆ Holy ground when I'm filled with shame.

◆ Holy ground when I'm gripped with condemnation.

◆ Holy ground—a divine encounter. At the
moment of my greatest need, He is there.

And then God says, "I have surely seen the affliction of my people which are in Egypt, and have heard
their cry by reason of their taskmasters; for I know
their sorrows."—Exodus 3:7, KJV.

Are you going through some sorrow in your life?
Going through some disappointment? God says, "I
know your sorrows. I'm with you in your agony. I'm
there in the depths of your disappointment. I'm there
through your isolated, lonely nights.

"I'm there when you put your head on your pillow
and cry yourself to sleep because of your kids. I'm
there when you are weeping in the night because of
your broken marriage. I'm there when you wonder,
'Why God—why me? Why was I afflicted with cancer? Why me, God?'

"I'm there when you feel unbearably lonely and isolated. I'm there in your shame. I'm there in your condemnation when you don't live up to the divine ideal
and you feel so dirty and guilty."

God says, "I'm there. I'm there in the bush. I'm
there, and I know your sorrows, your disappointments."

And then God said: "Moses, I AM THAT I AM
. . . . Thus shalt thou say unto the children of Israel, I
AM hath sent me unto you."—Exodus 3:14, KJV.

"Moses, you're ready now. Kneeling before Me in
shame and guilt, opening your heart for My forgiveness, you are ready, and I AM THAT I AM."

What does it mean when God says "I AM THAT I
AM"?

He was saying to Moses, "I AM your strength. I AM your sufficiency. I AM your courage. I AM your nourishment. I AM your pillar of fire by night. I AM your cloud of protection by day. I AM your covering. I AM your guide. I AM all that you need."

And when I come to Him in my own wilderness wandering, it becomes a divine encounter, because I meet Him at the bush. And He says, "I AM all that you need. I AM the love you didn't receive as a child. I AM the forgiveness for your guilt. I AM the power for deliverance in your life. I AM your nourishment for the inner loneliness of your soul. I AM all that your heart needs. I AM that I AM."

When we wander from Him and run from Him, when we turn our backs on Him, at times we meet Him in a divine encounter in the wilderness. When we feel that our plans are gone, God Himself takes our wilderness wanderings and turns them into divine encounters.

Moses was humbled by need—but need is the material for miracles.

God's ultimate goal was to lead Moses to a place of dependence on Him. And one way God does that is by bringing us to a place of need! Needs are opportunities for miracles. Miracles come out of need. Where there is no need, there is no miracle. Where there is no need, there is no supernatural event. Scripture describes the miracle manna. God turns needs into miracles.

"And the whole congregation of the children of Israel murmured against Moses and Aaron in the wilderness: And the children of Israel said unto them, Would to God we had died by the hand of the Lord in the land of Egypt, when we sat by the fleshpots."
—Exodus 16:2, KJV.

Look, Moses, at least in Egypt our taskmasters gave us something to eat so that we could make those bricks without straw. Look, Moses, at least when we were in Egypt, our stomachs were full. But you've brought us out into the wilderness to die.

God teaches us dependence when we have a need. Needs are the stuff miracles are made of.

The Israelites felt a need. Do you have some need? The need to be loved? Some financial need in your life? Do you have some need today?

Where there is sight, there is no need for a miracle to be healed of blindness. The fact that I'm blind physically means that I need sight. Jesus didn't heal people from blindness who were not blind. He healed people who had a need to see. Where there was no withered arm, there was no need to heal an arm that was not withered. Where there is no need, there is no need for a miracle.

So every need that you have in your life that you cannot fulfill, every need you have that's impossible for you to figure out, there is a need for God. If you could solve all your own problems, there would be no need for God. If there were no difficulties in life and you pretty well had your arms around everything, where would God fit in? So God allows us in life to face needs, difficulties, obstacles, mountains, tunnels that we don't see any way out of.

And His miracles occur in the context of human need. When you bring human need together with faith and commitment, the way is open for God to work a miracle.

"Then said the Lord unto Moses, Behold, I will rain bread from heaven for you; and the people shall go out and gather a certain rate every day. . . . And in the morning, then shall ye see the glory of the Lord."—Exodus 16:4, 7, KJV.

Moses, the best is yet to come. Moses, in the context of your need, in the context of hunger, the best is yet to come.

I thank the Lord that in the context of our need, God works miracles. I thank the Lord that there is a God who satisfies every need we have or ever will have.

Do you have a need today in your life?

◆ A need in your marriage?

◆ A need for help with your kids?

◆ A need with your finances?

◆ A need with your health?

God doesn't rain down manna when you've just gone through a buffet and your stomach is filled.

If the Israelites were going through Egyptian buffets picking the wrong stuff from the buffets, they would never have seen the manna rain down from heaven. We see the manna fall when we're hungry, and we see God meet the need when we *need*. So need is not to discourage me. Need is not to disappoint me. Need is not to cause me to have a lack of faith. Need is to cause me to reach up to Him who is the solution to the need.

◆ He turns curses into blessings. The best is yet to come.

◆ In my wilderness wanderings I have divine encounters. The best is yet to come.

◆ When I have a need, that's stuff that miracles are made out of. The best is yet to come.

And when our fondest dreams are smashed, when our greatest hopes dance away like a shadow and when life is over—I don't mean death at the end—but when something inside us dies and we say I can never fulfill my dreams, consider Moses.

Moses was disciplined at death—but when our dreams die, God's are born.

Moses comes to the end. Life is over. Life is finished. Life is gone. He has lived for one thing. He's old now. Taught twelve years by his mother, educated forty years in the schools of Egypt, then through forty more years wandering in the wilderness, he's now on the borders of the Promised Land. He's old now. His face is weather-beaten; his eyes deep-set. He's been through trial after trial, focused on but one goal: "Lord, before I die, let me put my feet in the Promised Land. Before I die, Lord, let me eat of the fruit of Jericho.

Before I die, Lord, let me taste the land of milk and honey. And Lord, let me not die in the wilderness. Lord, let me die in the Promised Land. Let met die with the hope and assurance of the Promised Land."

And Moses approaches the Promised Land. He looks from the mountaintops, across the Jezreel valley, and into Jericho. He sees the Promised Land!

"So Moses the servant of the Lord died there in the land of Moab."—Deuteronomy 34:5, KJV.

No, God—no! Not in the land of Moab. Not among the heathen—among those who don't know You. Not among the idol worshipers. God, I have one hope. I have one dream. God, let me die in the Promised Land.

"So Moses the servant of the Lord died there in the land of Moab, according to the word of the Lord. And he buried him in a valley in the land of Moab, over against Beth-pe-or: but no man knoweth of his sepulchre unto this day."—Deuteronomy 34:5, 6, KJV.

Moses had a dream, but the best was yet to come, because God had a better dream. Moses had a plan, but God had a better plan. Moses had a goal, but God had a better goal.

Jesus, as it's told in Jude 9—the all-powerful Christ—argues with Satan about the body of Moses. Jesus resurrects Moses. He takes him, but not to the earthly Promised Land to die—for his bones to decay and bleach, for his flesh to rot, to remain in a tomb for thousands of years until the Second Coming. That was not God's plan. That was not God's goal.

God's goal was to resurrect Moses right then and take him to heaven as a token and type of all those who will be resurrected. Moses' plan had to fail so that God's plan would succeed. Moses' dream had to die so that God's dream could be born. God had something much better for Moses. It's better to be in heaven than to be in the grave. And God took Moses there, because God can do exceedingly, abundantly above what we ask or think.

When your dreams are broken, when your plans are shattered, when your goals are crushed, the best is yet to come. Because in Jesus, there is no failure. In Jesus, there is no defeat. In Jesus, there is no permanent setback. For Moses, it was home at last, because the best is yet to come.

One day we shall live in a land where there is no sickness or sorrow or defeat or suffering or pain.

One day we shall see Him face to face, feel His warm embrace, experience His presence, and shout, "Home at last! Home at last! Home at last!"

For the best is yet to come!

TEN

I need to look to Jesus—who can
satisfy all my deepest needs.

Jesus Satisfies Our Every Need

WHAT IS IT ABOUT JESUS that meets the
most urgent inner needs of our souls? How does He
satisfy our heart's most fervent longings?

Here are four ways Jesus satisfies our deepest needs:

First, God both shows us and tells us that **we matter to Him**—that we are special and important. He
created us. We're not merely skin covering bones.
We're not a random combination of chemicals. He loves
each of us individually.

*Looking to Jesus, I
discover that all my
restless longings and
deepest inner needs are
met—and I am fully
satisfied!*

Deep, inner, lasting satisfaction comes from knowing that
the Creator of the universe
loves me with an incredible
love. I matter to Him. I am
valuable in His sight.

Second, God not only created us, but **He has a plan
for our life.** He is always planning the very best for

us. Jeremiah the prophet declares, "For I know the thoughts that I think toward you, saith the Lord, thoughts of peace, and not of evil, to give you an expected end."—Jeremiah 29:11, KJV. In spite of life's ups and downs, God has a plan. In spite of life's disappointments and sorrows, God is working all things out for my good. (See Romans 8:28.)

Third, enduring inner satisfaction comes from knowing that **the grace of Christ is greater than all our failures.** In Christ there is forgiveness and freedom from guilt. In Christ there is mercy and pardon.

The apostle John states, "For God did not send His Son into the world to condemn the world, but that the world through Him might be saved."—John 3:17, NKJV. The apostle Paul adds, "There is therefore now no condemnation to those who are in Christ Jesus."—Romans 8:1, NKJV. There is no greater inner satisfaction than in knowing that Christ doesn't condemn you.

Fourth, the greatest satisfaction of all is in knowing that one day **Jesus will make a complete, total, and utter end of sin.** Jesus will return. Sickness, suffering, and sorrow will be no more. Disease, disaster, and death will be over. Worry, want, and war will be forever banished. "And God will wipe away every tear from their eyes; there shall be no more death, nor sorrow, nor crying. There shall be no more pain, for the former things have passed away."—Revelation 21:4, NKJV.

In Jesus, our heart's longings will soon be forever filled. In Him, our soul's desires will be eternally satisfied. In Him, we are complete. Now that's something to sing about. It's time to rejoice! ▲